LAND GIRL

LAND
GIRL

A MANUAL FOR VOLUNTEERS
IN THE WOMEN'S LAND ARMY

1941

W.E.SHEWELL-COOPER

AMBERLEY

This edition first published 2011

Amberley Publishing Plc
Cirencester Road, Chalford,
Stroud, Gloucestershire, GL6 8PE

www.amberleybooks.com

British Library Cataloguing in Publication Data.
A catalogue record for this book is available from the British Library.

ISBN 978 1 4456 0279 0

Typesetting and Origination by Amberley Publishing.
Printed in Great Britain.

CONTENTS

FOREWORD

By The Lady Denman, D.B.E.
(Honorary Director of the Women's Land Army.)

Germany is attempting to starve the British people into submission. To win the war, our country must defeat the blockade. This is the joint task of the British Navy and of Britain's great field force of agricultural workers.

The Women's Land Army was organised in readiness three months before the outbreak of hostilities. The calling up of men from the land has been slow and the growth of the Land Army correspondingly gradual. Farmers' memories are short, and in spite of the good work done on the land by women during the last war, the Land Army has had to encounter much prejudice against the employment of women's labour. This prejudice has now almost everywhere been overcome through the really magnificent service given by the first few thousand employed volunteers who worked through the bitter winter of 1939 under conditions of great difficulty and loneliness and have stuck to their jobs ever since. To these volunteers and the many others with the same fine spirit now working in the Land Army the country owes a great deal.

The Land Army is now ten thousand strong, and the demand for new volunteers is great and urgent. Men are beginning to go from the land into the fighting services; huge new tracts of land are being ploughed up to produce food for the people of this country and feeding-stuffs for stock. Every acre of pasture that goes under the plough means a demand for additional labour.

I commend the Women's Land Army to all readers of this handbook as one of the most vitally important forms of war service open to women. There is a place in the Land Army to-day for every young woman who is fit and strong, who cares for country things and prefers hard work and long hours in the open air to hard work and long hours in the factory, who is ready to go where she is needed and who means to stick to her job, without weakening or grumbling or turning back, until the war is over. The Land Army fights in the fields. It is in the fields of Britain that the most critical battle of the present war may well be fought and won.

CHAPTER I

THE WOMEN'S LAND ARMY IN THE GREAT WAR, 1914–18

By Dame Meriel Talbot, D.B.E.

It was not until the third year of the Great War (1917) that the first Women's Land Army was formed.

Before then certain steps had been taken by unofficial Societies, and in 1916 by the Government, to encourage women to come forward from their village homes and elsewhere to help the farmers— I was myself appointed in 1916 by the Minister of Agriculture (Lord Selborne) to advise and co-operate with the Ministry in this matter. But with the increasing destruction of food-laden ships by the enemy, and the consequent need for production of more food at home, together with the withdrawal of men and more men from the farms, Mr. Prothero (later Lord Ernle), Minister of Agriculture in 1917, made an important decision. He chose to create

a precedent rather than to follow one. He appointed a new branch in his Ministry to ensure a
large and steady supply of women labour for the
farms. He decided that the branch was to be
staffed entirely by women, and under a Director to
be responsible to him as Minister. 1917 was a
sombre year for our country. I recall Mr. Prothero's saying at that time, " England is like a
beleaguered city." There was only about three
weeks' food supply in the country. The need for a
mobile force of women to supplement the part-time
workers, to go anywhere and give their help where
and when it was wanted became apparent—thus the
Women's Land Army came into being in 1917.

At first the main difficulties to be met and overcome were six-fold :—

1. *The Source of Supply.*—The other women's
Services—V.A.D.s,   W.A.A.C.s.,   W.R.E.N.s,
W.A.A.F.s.—had already absorbed a large number
of girls : the supply had been combed out fairly
thoroughly.

2. *The Scepticism of the Farmers*—and indeed of
the public generally.

3. *The Problem of the Waiting Time*—*e.g.*,
between the short training or, more accurately,

testing, and employment; or, again, when weather or seasonal conditions interrupted employment.

4. *The Wages to be Given.*—It should be remembered that, unlike the other War Services, whose members were the servants of the Service concerned, employed and paid by the same, the members of the Women's Land Army were enrolled and equipped by the Government, but depended on the individual farmer for employment—and payment. In order to safeguard the girl, and to ensure against her employment as a form of cheap labour, a minimum wage was soon authorised by the Ministry.

5. *The Question of Billeting.*

6. *The Loneliness of Farm Work.*—Here again there is a marked difference from the conditions in the other Services, where women work and live together.

As to organisation, a beginning had already been made by the then Board of Trade to appoint Women's Agriculture Committees in each county. This was developed and completed. County offices were opened and Organising Secretaries appointed. Then followed the appointment of Travelling Inspectors to supervise the work in areas, and of Group Leaders in the villages. From the solitary woman officer first appointed to the

Ministry in 1916 developed a staff of many women,
both at the Ministry and in the country. Special
sections dealt with (*a*) Training and Hostels;
(*b*) County Organisation; (*c*) Equipment (tunic,
breeches, gaiters, boots, hat); (*d*) Propaganda.
(It must be remembered that at that time there was
no wireless; the need for recruits and the oppor-
tunities offered had to be made known through
the Press, and by open-air rallies and meetings in
London and throughout the country.)

Publications.—Besides official leaflets, a monthly
magazine, *The Landswoman,* was edited and produced by the Women's Branch. It did much to
mitigate the loneliness of many girls and to keep
alive the corporate inspiration.

All this had to be carried through at breakneck
speed, with no precedent and no time for preparation. The Prime Minister, Mr. Lloyd George—
himself an inspiring hustler at that time—decided
to get a " move on " at the Ministry. He organised
the new Food Production Department within its
stately walls, with Sir Arthur Lee (later Lord Lee
of Fareham) as Director, and put the Women's
Branch under its control.

On the top of this large, hastily planned organisation came the responsibility of the Women's Branch for guiding and developing the Women's Institute organisation, then in its early childhood. It is of interest to recall that I was able to enlist the services of Lady Denman as one of the staff of the Women's Institute Section in the Ministry, and later to hand the growing movement back to her care as Chairman of the National Federation, and to acclaim her as the Hon. Director of the present Women's Land Army.

Ultimately some 45,000 young women applied to enrol. Of this number about 50 per cent. was rejected by the Selection Panels set up throughout the country. We were confident that nothing would be more damaging to the whole enterprise than the girl who could not or would not " stick it ". About 23,000 were ultimately enrolled, and in spite of human limitations and failures here and there, they certainly gave a good account of themselves.

To-day we know what London courage means. Twenty-three years ago it was from the London girls in the Women's Land Army that we learnt to expect most skill and courage. As to the work achieved by this new body of young women, I would quote from my recent letter to *The Times*:—

" The returns (from a survey taken in 1918 of 12,637 Land Army Members) showed that the work was distributed as follows: 5734 milkers, 293 tractor-drivers, 3971 field workers, 635 carters, 260 ploughmen, 84 thatchers, 21 shepherds. Lord Ernle, a recognised authority on British farming, was Minister of Agriculture at that time. Writing shortly after the Armistice he said: ' The branches which have been enumerated (in the Survey) have covered a wide field. In all of them women have excelled. . . . In driving motor-tractors they have done at least as well as men. Here also light hands tell. As drivers they have shown themselves not only skilful and enduring, but economical.' "

After the Land Army was disbanded in 1919, many of the members took advantage of the free passage to the Dominions offered to ex-service men and women. Others continued in farm or garden work at home, or became farm owners themselves. Many married countrymen, and doubtless a large number returned to their former occupations.

CHAPTER II

THE NEED OF THE LAND ARMY TODAY

NEVER before has the country faced such a cruel, merciless enemy. Hitler is undoubtedly out to starve the nation, and he has said so publicly, in no uncertain words. His U-boat campaign is launched for that purpose, and for that purpose only.

He knows perfectly well that Germany lost the last war largely through the blockade, and he is determined to do all he can to blockade us. It is therefore of the greatest importance to see that this country becomes more and more self-supporting.

Although gardeners and allotment-holders will do, and are doing, a great deal to increase food production, the burden of food-growing is bound to fall on to the farmers, fruit-growers and market-gardeners of the country.

It is no use blaming past Governments or sitting down and wringing one's hands now. Everyone knows that we have been relying on millions of tons of vegetables, grain, meat and other produce coming from abroad. Past history must be past history, and we have got to face the future with confidence— a confidence born of our determination to do better henceforth.

Because of the agricultural depression, and because we were satisfied to allow other countries to feed us, English farming developed in peace-time on the cheapest lines possible.

A farm the author knows very well in Warwickshire, which runs to an extent of nearly 1000 acres, was farmed for years in peace-time by the farmer himself, his wife, a man and a boy—grass, grass, nothing but pastures with sheep grazing thereon. But the War Agricultural Committee has now come along and has said that that farmer must plough up some 250 acres, and next year an additional 200, so the farmer, who was quite content with one man and a boy to help him, is now crying out for more labour.

This kind of thing can be multiplied several hundreds of times—nay, probably thousands of times—all over the country: grass being ploughed up, with the consequence of more labour needed.

In addition to this, there is the greater intensification of cropping: the market-gardener who might be satisfied with a simple cropping scheme in peace-time is trying—quite rightly, too—to intensify his production; and the more intensive the production, the more labour is required.

It will be seen, therefore, that there is a great need for the Women's Land Army in this war, which we must win. Not only do the Land Girls take the place of men who have been called to the colours, or of workers who have had to go, for one reason or another, to other work; but they are needed, and vitally needed, to amplify the labour that is available in the countryside at the present time.

There always have been in peace-time thousands of women and girls working on the land, and it is not desired to recruit these into the Women's Land Army. They are asked to go on doing their important work; they are asked to remain in the villages where they live, and to work harder than ever. The Women's Land Army needs women from other professions, women from all walks of life, women who are anxious to help their country in a time of need and who are attracted to the open

B

air. The Land Army member is bound to be mobile. She is willing to go where she is sent.

It is hoped, therefore, that it is quite clear that the Women's Land Army is not for those who are already employed in agriculture, but for the volunteers who are willing to make agriculture their war-time profession.

Some 12,000 women have already enrolled in this magnificent Army, led by the Honorary Director, the Lady Denman, D.B.E. It is hoped that as a result of this book thousands more will join, for work on the land is a form of national service of incalculable benefit to the country at the present time.

Listen to part of the message of the Rt. Hon. R. S. Hudson, P.C., M.P., the Minister of Agriculture and Fisheries, to the Women's Land Army in October 1940. He said :—

" The events of the past 6 months have made increased food production at home even more urgent. Total war is a war of endurance, and to ensure winning it we must make the most use of all our resources, especially the land. Milking the cows, feeding the pigs and the poultry or driving a tractor, day after day, is unspectacular and at times may seem to you very dull.

" But without the food you help to produce the bravery of the fighting services would be of no avail and the machinery in our munition factories would be silent and still. Famine could achieve what no bomb or blitzkrieg or invading force will ever bring about. It is your vital task to see that such a thing could in no conceivable circumstance arise, and is driven even further from the realms of possibilities."

CHAPTER III

HOW TO JOIN

BEFORE starting on this chapter proper may I put two personal suggestions to readers?

1. If *you* were in the Land Army at the beginning of the war, and have been trained, and were doing well in the job, but had to resign for private reasons, do apply again now, if you are free, for you are badly needed.

2. Many women enrolled at the beginning of the war. Some of their forms may have been lost through enemy action or some other war emergency. If you are one of those who have never had a reply to the original form you filled in, do apply immediately to the County Secretary, whose address you will find in Chapter IX.

Now for prospective members.

Enrolment full-time mobile volunteers accepted only.

Only volunteers who can offer full-time mobile service (that is, service in any part of the country) are accepted for enrolment in the Women's Land Army. Volunteers are placed, as first choice, in employment in their county of enrolment, if employment offers there. They are only asked to go farther afield if no local employment offers *or* if the need for their services is greater elsewhere.

Application Forms

Each applicant for enrolment is required to complete application form No. W.L.A. E. & W. 1. (See Form A.)

Interviewing

Applicants, who should be women of good physique between the ages of 18 and 40 (except in very special cases), are interviewed by members of the Land Army panel of interviewers for the county, and if considered suitable for service on the land, are accepted and formally enrolled.

On being accepted, volunteers are required to sign a form of undertaking (see Form B) that they will hold themselves available for service on the land during the period of the war, unless unforeseen

A

APPLICATION FOR ENROLMENT

This application should be completed and sent to the Organising Secretary, Women's Land Army County Committee

(For Secretary, see p. 85.)

SECTION I.—For Use by Applicant.

(1) Surname...
   (In Block Letters and stating whether Mrs. or Miss)

(2) Christian Names ....
....

(3) Age ....

(4) Full home address ....
....

(5) Present occupation ....

(6) Usual occupation if unemployed or if different from that shown under (5).
....

(7) If employed, state Employer's name and address.
   (If own employer, state " on own account ")
....

(8) Employer's business...

Signature of applicant...
   (Additional particulars may be entered here)

---

circumstances make this impossible. They are also required to produce a satisfactory medical certificate (see Form C).

No volunteer has to give up her employment until definitely notified by the Land Army that she is needed.

Sometimes a preliminary interview will take place in the volunteer's home by the local representative, this being followed by a formal interview at the County Office or some other convenient place. It must be understood that even if the medical certificate shows fitness, the volunteer may not be accepted if the interviewers think that she is of poor physique or is not sufficiently strong to carry out Land Army work.

The interview is neither formal nor frightening, and the interviewers are merely out to discover the capabilities and possibilities of the candidates. The kind of questions interviewers ask are as follows:—

1. Have you had any experience of agriculture or horticulture?

2. Have you any preference for any particular work?

(E & W) 2.   FORM OF UNDERTAKING   **B**

I hereby accept registration as a member of the Women's Land Army and promise to hold myself available for service on the land for the period of the war subject to the conditions laid down for the training and employment of the Women's Land Army.

I realise that, should circumstances arise which prevent my carrying out this promise, I must ask the Secretary of the Women's Land Army for the County in which I am then residing for permission to resign and must, on receiving this permission, return my uniform and my badge.

Signed ....

Name (Block Letters) ....
(State whether Mrs. or Miss)

*Permanent address ....

....

* The Women's Land Army Secretary for the County should be notified of any change of permanent address.

22

MEDICAL CERTIFICATE

C

WOMEN'S LAND ARMY

NAME OF VOLUNTEER .... W.L.A. No.............

ADDRESS ....

Members of the Women's Land Army must be capable of arduous and sustained physical labour in all weathers and a general certificate to this effect is required in the case of each volunteer.

GENERAL CERTIFICATE :—

I have examined $\frac{\text{Mrs.}}{\text{Miss}}$ .... and certify that

she is in good health and is suffering from no disability* that would be likely to make her unfit for work on the land under the conditions mentioned above.

Signature...

Place......................................

Date ....

* Please note below any specific disability (*e.g.* deafness, bad eyesight, etc.) or any condition below normal which may make a recruit unsuitable for a particular post (*e.g.* tractor driver or a post of individual responsibility) but which is not necessarily sufficient to justify rejection.

....

....

23

3. What size of uniform do you require?

4. What is your present occupation?

5. Can you drive a car? Can you ride a bicycle?

6. Have you had any experience of country life?

7. Will you please produce the names and addresses of two references, private or business?

Membership Cards

When the Form of Undertaking has been signed and a satisfactory medical certificate produced, the volunteer will be presented with her Women's Land Army badge and her membership card, which serves as a reminder of the obligations she has undertaken.

At the same time the Women's Land Army make out what is known as a Case Sheet, which serves as a history of the volunteer and gives her record of service.

Transfers

It is possible for a volunteer to transfer from one county to another, but this is not welcomed unless there is some very definite reason for doing so.

If a volunteer finds employment for herself in a county other than her county of enrolment or previous employment, she must pay her own travelling expenses as far as the border of her new county of employment.

Resignations and Dismissals

It is possible for a volunteer to resign for urgent private reasons or for reasons of health.

Volunteers, however, are reminded that money has been spent on them to make them specialists for a vital job, so they should never resign unless it is *absolutely* necessary: " You are feeding the nation; if *you* drop out, someone may starve."

If a volunteer proves unsatisfactory she may be discharged. In a necessitous case it is usual to pay the volunteer's fare home, or a travelling warrant is issued.

The reasons for dismissal from the Women's Land Army will normally be:—

1. Unsuitable conduct, or
2. Repeated dismissal from employment, or
3. Refusal to resign, although invited to do so.

On dismissal or resignation the volunteer will

have to return forthwith her Women's Land Army badge and the Women's Land Army outfit and uniform.

In special cases of resignation the volunteer may be allowed to keep the armlet.

CHAPTER IV

TRAINING (IF NECESSARY)

VOLUNTEERS may be given training if the County Secretaries feel that they need it, and this may be done either (*a*) on a farm, or (*b*) at a Training Centre (*i.e.*, at an Agricultural College or Farm Institute). If, however, the volunteer has had some experience, she may be sent straight into vital employment. It may be also that the volunteer will be considered suitable to go into some type of agricultural employment which does not necessitate special training.

In the case of *farm* training, this may be on the farm on which the volunteer is afterwards going to work, or it may be on a training farm, and then the volunteer will subsequently be passed on to another farm.

Payments and Allowances

Volunteers who are accepted for training are sent for four weeks for a free course, either at an approved farm or at an Agricultural College or Farm Institute.

Board and lodging is paid for by the Government, and an allowance at the rate of 10*s*. per week, less National Health and Unemployment Insurance contributions, is made by the Government to the volunteer for her personal expenses.

Training on Farms

The farmers who take trainees for instruction must, of course, be those who have time to spare to give such instruction. Volunteers on such farms can be assured that they will receive genuine training.

The training may be carried out on farms where the volunteer can be given special instruction in milking, tractor-driving, or the care of stock and poultry, or on those market-gardens and private gardens where all-round instruction can be given under supervision. The trainee will not simply be used for the purpose of providing unskilled labour, nor will she be expected to stick to only one or two processes.

The trainee should take with her her insurance cards and her ration books, containing the proper number of coupons.

The course of training normally starts on a

Monday, and at least one clear week before the training is due the volunteer will receive a form (see D) signed by the County Secretary.

On the second day of each week of training a claim form will be sent by the trainee to the Finance Section of the Women's Land Army Branch at the Ministry of Agriculture and Fisheries. Claim forms should be filled in correctly, and, to help trainees, notes will be supplied by the County Secretaries at the beginning of the training.

The billeting fees will be paid by the Government in a similar manner, and claim forms will be provided for the persons doing the billeting. When, however, the Women's Land Army trainee is living in her own home, or that of her parents, no weekly billeting fee will be paid. A fee up to 10s. per week may, however, be paid in such cases to the farmer if he is providing meals for the trainee.

National Health, Pensions and Unemployment Insurance

Members of the Women's Land Army placed in training come within the scope of the National Health Contributory pensions and Unemployment Schemes. Any trainee who has not already got her

MINISTRY OF AGRICULTURE AND FISHERIES

WOMEN'S LAND ARMY

Abroathshire County Secretary

Address *Roserobin Hall*

Syrinham,

Abroath.

NOTIFICATION OF TRAINING

Dear Madam,

A 4-weeks' training starting on Monday *the 1st inst.* has been arranged for you, as an enrolled member of the Women's Land Army, with *Mr. Edward Brown,* at *Copsacks Farm, Little Puddleton.*

During training, you will be billeted at *Mrs. R. Rogers, Rose Cottage, Snag Lane, Little Puddleton.* The nearest station is *Crowton, L.N.E.R.,* and you should arrive on *the 31st instant.*

You must notify the farmer of the exact date and time of your arrival as soon as possible after receiving this letter.

During training, your board and lodging will be provided free, and in addition a personal allowance of 10/- per week less National Health and Unemployment Insurance contributions will be made to you. Four forms are enclosed on which this allowance should be claimed by you each week. When sending your claim for the first week's allowance, you *must* enclose your National Health and Unemployment Insurance cards, which will be stamped and returned to you with your personal allowance for the fourth week of training. When sending up your insurance cards, please be sure to state the *date and year of your birth.*

OVER

C

I have received your letter and {*will / *am unable to} report for training as instructed. I am notifying the farmer immediately of my time of arrival.

Signed *Winnie Gibbraith*

W.L.A. No. *3715621*

Cross out the words which do no apply.

If you have not already got insurance cards, you can obtain a National Health Insurance card from a Post Office and an Unemployment Insurance card from any Employment Exchange.

A form is also enclosed on which you may claim a refund of your travelling expenses to your place of training. This form should be sent in with the claim for the personal allowance for your first week of training.

Please note that your training has been arranged on the understanding that compensation will be paid to you by the Minister of Agriculture and Fisheries in respect of any accident arising out of and during the course of your training and that you agree not to take proceedings or make any claim for damages against the person training you.

A Land Army working outfit is available for your use during training and *you may have this by applying to the County Office personally—or if you prefer we will send this by post*. In addition you should take ordinary clothes, underclothes and personal necessities, including your Ration Book.

The note at the foot of the first page should be detached and filled in by you and sent to me at the address at the head of this letter by return of post.

32

I hope you will be satisfied with your training arrangements and that a post on this or on some other farm will result, always provided your training report is satisfactory. In case of any difficulty, please apply to :

Yours faithfully,

(Mrs.) *Georgina Fallser.*
County Secretary.

Abroathshire

" cards " should obtain the Health Insurance card from a post office and the unemployment card from the Employment Exchange.

The cards will be stamped at the Ministry, and the trainee's share of the contributions deducted from the weekly payment of personal allowance. The cards must be forwarded to the Ministry with the first week's claim.

Reports

The farmer is given a report to fill in (see E), which he completes at the end of the third week of training and sends to the County Secretary.

Travelling Expenses

The Women's Land Army trainee will be given travelling warrant by the County Secretary for the rail journey to the farm. Any bus-travelling which has to be done in addition to, or instead of, the rail journey will be paid for, as will the cost of sending luggage in advance. A separate form has to be used for this. These expenses must *not* be put on the personal allowance claim form.

Special Notes

Inform your County Secretary *immediately*:—

(*a*) If the date when you begin your training is changed.

(*b*) If there is a change in the name of your billetor, and the date of change.

(*c*) If you leave before the four weeks' training is over.   State date and why.

(*d*) If you are unable to continue because of illness or accident.

(*e*) If the accident is due directly to your training.   (In this case it may be possible to make a claim for compensation to the Ministry of Agriculture.)

(*f*) If you are in any difficulty at all.

Training at Centres

A volunteer sent to a Training Centre must be prepared, on completing training, to accept work in any part of the country where her services are needed.   Trainees will normally pass into immediate employment at the end of the four weeks' training course.   They may, on the other hand, remain at the College or Farm Institute for a further few days, if this is likely to make it easier to place them in employment.   Normally they will not stay for more than one additional week.

E

MINISTRY OF AGRICULTURE AND FISHERIES

WOMEN'S LAND ARMY

Dear ....   Name.................................

W.L.A. No.............

The above member of the Women's Land Army has been informed that a course of training on your farm has been arranged for her for the period from

.... to ....

She has been instructed to notify you of the time of her arrival.

When she has finished her third week of training, I should be very much obliged if you would complete and return to me the form of report below, which will be treated as confidential.

Yours very truly,

Secretary .... County Committee.

Address ....

36

FARMER'S REPORT

W.L.A. No. ....   Name ....

1. Date on which training started ....

2. Did you find this volunteer

    (1) Strong enough for farm work ....

    (2) Handy ....

    (3) Willing and anxious to learn ....

3. While on your farm has she received instruction in :—

    Dairy work .... No. of Cows trainee can milk ....

    Poultry ....

    Care of Livestock ....

    Field Work ....

    Market Gardening ....

4. Please add any further remarks about the volunteer.

Signature of Farmer ....

At the College or Institute the weekly personal allowance is paid by the Head of the Training Centre. Ration and identity cards must, of course, be taken by the volunteer who is to be trained.

Insurance Cards, etc.

The insurance cards (see page 29, re Training on Farm) will be stamped at the Training Centre, and the volunteer's share of the contributions deducted from her personal allowance. At the end of the training the cards will be handed back to the trainee.

Where a volunteer is to be trained at a Farm Institute she will receive a notification of training on a green form (see F).

Training Centre Report

As in the case of farm-training, the Training Centre will issue a report on the trainee as per form G below.

Unemployment Benefit and Assistance

Trainees either at farms or at Training Centres are not eligible during the period of training either for unemployment benefit or assistance, but any title to such benefit acquired before the period of training will not be adversely affected by the training period.

If (but this is now very unlikely) members of the Women's Land Army cannot find employment after their period of training, they can claim unemployment benefit or assistance.

Special Training—Timber Measurers

Special training is offered to those who are fitted to become timber measurers (see page 61). This training is provided at the Forestry Commission School in the Forest of Dean, under the usual Women's Land Army conditions. After such training, volunteers are assured, if satisfactory, of immediate employment at a starting wage of 45*s.* per week.

Accident Compensation and Third-Party Risks

As has already been suggested, the Ministry of Agriculture is prepared to pay compensation in respect of any accident arising out of and during the course of Land Army training. Such payments are made *ex gratia*, for there is no legal liability on

MINISTRY OF AGRICULTURE AND FISHERIES

WOMEN'S LAND ARMY

Sloanshire County Secretary

Address *The White Manor*

Bakertown

Sloanshire

NOTIFICATION OF TRAINING

Dear Madam,

You, as an enrolled member of the Women's Land Army, are now asked to report for training at *The Sloanshire Farm Institute Batters-field, L.M.S.*, and you should arrive on **1st March.** The nearest station is *Batters-field, L.M.S.*, and you should arrive on **1st March.** The course will last **4 weeks.**

Your travelling (3rd Class) expenses will be refunded to you on arrival.

During training your board and lodging will be provided free, and in addition a personal allowance of 10/- a week, less National Health and Unemployment Insurance contributions, will be paid to you during training.

You must take with you when you report for training your National Health and Unemployment Insurance cards, which should be handed in on arrival. These will be returned to you at the end of your training. If you have not already got insurance cards, you can obtain a National Health Insurance card and a medical card through a Post Office and an Unemployment Insurance card from any Employment Exchange.

[OVER

I have received your letter and ${*\text{will} \atop *\text{am unable to}}$ report for training as instructed.

Signed *Tulipa Swanscombe*

W.L.A. No. *333777*

* Cross out the words which do not apply.

I enclose a form of Medical Certificate which you should have completed and signed by a doctor and take with you when you report for training.

A Land Army working outfit is available for your use during training and *will be given to you before you arrive at the Farm Institute.* In addition you should take ordinary clothes, underclothes and personal necessities, including your Ration Book.

Please note that your training has been arranged on the understanding that compensation will be paid to you by the Minister of Agriculture and Fisheries in respect of any accident arising out of and during the course of your training and that you agree not to take proceedings or make any claim for damages against the person training you.

Whilst we cannot guarantee that following training you will obtain immediate employment, every effort will be made to assist you in finding a post, always provided that your training report is satisfactory. If suitable employment offers at the end of your training, you will be expected to go direct to the farm where you will be employed.

The note at the foot of the first page should be detached and filled in by you and sent to me at the above address by return of post.

Yours faithfully,

(Miss) Harmonia Hedgebanks
County Secretary.

42

the Ministry to make them. Broadly speaking, payment will be based on the earnings of the trainee in her previous paid employment. Ordinary medical expenses will, of course, come under the National Health Insurance scheme.

Compensation is paid on the understanding that the trainee agrees not to take proceedings nor to make any claim for damages against the person training her.

The Ministry of Agriculture is also prepared to accept liability in regard to third-party risks in respect of accidents arising out of and in the course of Land Army training in cases where the farmer is not already covered against such risks by his normal insurances.

Women's Land Army volunteers should always apply to the County Secretary if they need any advice in this connection, and should report to the County Secretary any accident which arises during training.

Illness of Trainees

It is hoped that it is quite clear that a Women's Land Army trainee is entitled to free medical attention immediately on becoming insured, and so

MINISTRY OF AGRICULTURE AND FISHERIES

WOMEN'S LAND ARMY

Report from *Sloanshire Farm Institute* Training Centre.

Name of Trainee *Tulipa Swanscombe*

Date of commencement of training **1st March**

W.L.A. No. *333777*

County of Enrolment *Sloanshire*

Age 20

1. Subject(s) in which trainee has specialised.

~~Dairy work, including milking.~~
Tractor driving.
~~Poultry.~~

~~Pigs.~~
Horticulture.
~~Care of Livestock.~~

G

44

2. Aptitude for work.

   (a) Physical fitness   *Very Good*

   (b) Intelligence and general education *Excellent*

   (c) Keenness and adaptability *First rate*

   (d) Degree of proficiency acquired during training *1st Class*

3. Remarks.*

   A very good girl indeed. Has done a week's tractor ploughing and is mechanically minded.

* If milking included, state number of cows volunteer can milk and whether machine and/or hand milker.

In case of Tractor driving, give practical ploughing experience and extent of mechanical knowledge, if any.

Signed *R. B. Brownlow*   Date *April 3, 1941*
        Principal

she should take steps to get a medical card (if she has not already got one), join an approved society and *choose her panel doctor*. She should not wait till she is ill before doing this.

There is no need, though it is advisable, to join an approved Society, and those who do not wish to do so may obtain form Med. 50 from any Post Office (this is issued free), and, having filled it in, send it to the Insurance Committee for the Area.

On receipt of the medical card the trainee should fill up part A and take it to the doctor of her choice.

CHAPTER V

THE UNIFORM

Badges, clothing, personal clothing—What to take with
you.

EVERY member of the Women's Land Army, either
placed in training or in employment, is provided
free of charge with a smart uniform.   This uniform
consists of :—

(*a*) A serviceable rainproof mackintosh.

(*b*) A khaki overall coat.

(*c*) Two fawn shirts with turn-down collar.

(*d*) A pair of corduroy breeches.

(*e*) A pair of dungarees.

(*d*) A green knitted pullover.

(*g*) Three pairs of fawn stockings.

(*h*) A pair of heavy brown shoes.

(*i*) A pair of rubber gum boots.

(*j*) A brown felt hat.

(*k*) A green armlet with red royal crown on it.

(*l*) A badge of the " button-hole " type to wear
in civilian clothes (as illustrated below).

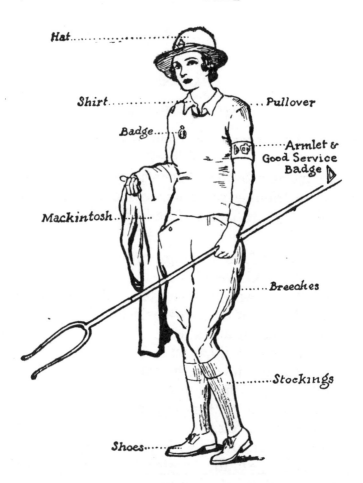

Hat

Shirt .... Pullover

Badge .... Armlet &
Good Service
Badge

Mackintosh

Breeches

Stockings

Shoes

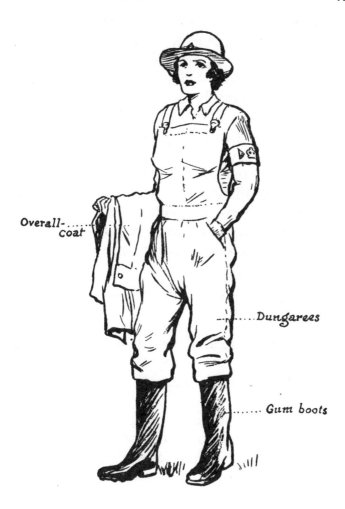

Overall-coat

Dungarees

Gum boots

Volunteers who are sent to work in districts with a particularly harsh climate, or who have to work under exposed conditions, receive in addition a warm form of woollen jumper known as a windcheater. Replacements of uniform are made at regular intervals.

The Women's Land Army naturally reserve the right to recover any such equipment if and when the volunteer ceases to become a member of this Army.

The drawing illustrates clearly the uniform and how it should be worn. Volunteers are asked to wear their hat correctly, and are reminded that a good volunteer is a good advertisement.

What to Take with You

In addition to the uniform, be sure to take with you :—

(*a*) Two complete sets of underclothes (at least).

(*b*) Two complete sets of night clothes (at least).

(*c*) A pair of house slippers.

(*d*) Another pair of walking-out shoes.

(*e*) One or two frocks for changing into in the evening.

(*f*) A woolly scarf to put round the head early in the morning.

(*g*) Woolly gloves.

(*h*) A bicycle, if you possess one.

(*i*) Ordinary toilet requisites.

Women's Land Army Badge

These are presented by the County Secretary to all volunteers who, after being interviewed, are thought suitable for enrolment in the Women's Land Army. If a volunteer loses her badge, a new one may be supplied for the sum of 6*d*.

Badges are also worn by Women's Land Army County Committees and official Organisers and by District Representatives.

Badges are recovered from volunteers and representatives who resign.

Good-Service Badges

Good-service badges, in the form of red half-diamonds outlined in green, are awarded to any volunteer who has completed six months' satisfactory service. The County Office decides whether the quality of the service justifies the award. Another half-diamond may be awarded at the end of the second six months' satisfactory service.

These half-diamonds are sown on to the armlet which is worn above the left elbow (see illustration, page 48).

Good-service badges can be replaced on payment of 6*d*., if adequate proof of the loss is furnished to the County Office concerned.

Special Notes on Uniform

Uniform replacements are made free of charge only when the County Office is satisfied that the old garment has been worn out by fair wear and tear. Hats, breeches, boots and mackintoshes are normally not replaced until the end of the year. Stockings are replaced at the end of six months, as also are gum boots, overall coats, pullovers and slipper socks.

The rules for replacement may be altered, and there are always exceptional cases where, owing to the particularly hard nature of the work, or weather conditions, replacements are made earlier.

Garments that are irreparably damaged owing to an accident due to no fault or negligence on the part of the volunteer are also replaced immediately.

Volunteers keep the old garments and use them to do the roughest work on the farm.

Receipts for Uniform

Every volunteer is required to sign a receipt on form W.L.A. U.7 for all items of uniform issued.

Women's Land Army Ties

Special ties are available to Land Army volunteers. These are sold at 1*s*. 9*d*., no extra charge being made for postage. These ties are particularly attractive, and are in Women's Land Army colours, with tiny Women's Land Army initials right across them in stripe form.

Pull-on Trousers

Volunteers may purchase pull-on trousers for their own use for the sum of 8*s*. per pair, post free. An order form may be obtained from County Headquarters, and this will be sent direct to Women's Land Army Headquarters, Balcombe Place, Balcombe, Sussex. Each order must be accompanied by a postal order or cheque for the correct amount, and this should be made payable to the Ministry of Agriculture, and not to any individual.

CHAPTER VI

EMPLOYMENT

Types of—Nature of work—Leave.

WOMEN are needed for all branches of work on the land. These branches include dairying and tending all types of livestock, general farm work, tractor-driving, work on fruit-farms and market-gardens, work in glasshouses, and work in private gardens which are given to the production of vegetables.

A certain number of volunteers are employed in forestry, both in the purely manual work of lopping and chopping timber and planting young trees, and in the more specialised branch of timber measurement, for which volunteers with secondary-school education are most suitable.

It must be clearly understood that members of the Women's Land Army are only available for employment in connection with food production. They are, therefore, never used on nurseries growing flowers, or in parks or private gardens, except where the latter have been entirely turned over to food production.

Sometimes the War Agricultural Committees employ members of the Women's Land Army to work in gangs hired out to farmers, but such Committees always promise to provide regular work for these gangs throughout the year.

There was a tendency at the beginning of the war for farmers to stand off Women's Land Army volunteers for a period during the winter months, but latterly farmers have been persuaded to keep the volunteers regularly employed the whole year round, and many a volunteer has done a tremendous amount of good work for her country by being used to clean out ditches and cut hedges during slack periods in the winter.

Sometimes, where they occupy land that is not being used for allotments, Urban or Rural District Councils become employers of Women's Land Army volunteers. They employ the labour for growing crops, and thus for helping to meet the nation's needs.

Conditions of Employment

Every enrolled Women's Land Army member is required to work under the conditions governing the wages and employment of the Women's Land

Army as a whole. No member may offer her services to a farmer on a voluntary basis. Workers who wish to work voluntarily on a farm cannot be members of the Women's Land Army.

Wages

The Ministry of Agriculture and Fisheries has laid down, as a condition of the employment of a member of the Women's Land Army, that she should be paid a weekly wage of not less than 32*s.* if she is 18 or over for a working week of up to 48 hours, with a minimum overtime rate of 8*d.* per hour. If she is billeted in the farmhouse, she must receive a minimum of 16*s.* per week in addition to free board and lodging. Of course, if the County wage rates are higher, higher wages are paid to the volunteer. In some counties, for instance, these are as high as 38*s.*

Before a volunteer goes on to the farm she will be told what is the working week and what is the county rate of wages. She will also be told whether Sunday labour and labour on days of public holiday are counted as ordinary overtime or as overtime on a higher scale.

Holidays

There are no special Women's Land Army regulations about holidays, with or without pay, but where a member of the Army has worked for six months at least 20 miles from her home she becomes entitled to a free journey home at the expense of the Women's Land Army (see Chapter VIII). A volunteer's title to the holiday, however, does depend on the terms of her employment and the arrangements that can be made with her employer.

Sickness and Accidents

Where a volunteer is employed on a weekly basis, the employer is expected to pay her wage in full if she is absent from work owing to sickness, and until he has given her a week's notice and this has expired.

There is no liability of any sort on the Ministry of Agriculture or on the Women's Land Army in respect of the sickness of a member or of any accident she may suffer while in employment.

Employed members of the Women's Land Army who fall sick are treated under the National Health Insurance Scheme (see page 29).

Where an accident occurs to an employed member of the Women's Land Army in the course of her employment, her claim is against her employer under the terms of the Workmen's Compensation Act. Medical treatment will, of course, be obtained under the National Health Insurance Scheme, and the worker will come within the Emergency Hospitals Scheme.

Billets and Accommodation

It is the responsibility of the employer to provide or arrange accommodation for his workers, and it is the duty of the County Secretary to satisfy herself that the accommodation offered is suitable, before agreeing to supply the labour.

Sometimes the farmer provides the meals in the farmhouse and lodging is made available elsewhere.

Neither the Ministry of Agriculture nor the Women's Land Army can be responsible for the debts of individual volunteers. It is the duty of the girl to pay her landlady regularly when she receives her wages.

In some cases a house is run as a hostel by the Women's Land Army for a group of workers working for several employers in the district, or the Y.W.C.A. may open a Residential Club or, where a number of volunteers are working for one employer, the employer may run a private hostel of his own.

Maintenance of Volunteers while Temporarily Unemployed

For not more than one month at any particular time or in any particular case, the County Office is authorised to maintain an unemployed Women's Land Army volunteer in a billet or hostel. The maintenance payment is limited to the cost of the board and lodging plus a small pocket-money allowance, usually 5s. per week.

This maintenance allowance is not a volunteer's right, but is a facility which keeps her readily available and near at hand for any new work that may come along. The payment for the billet in this case is, of course, done by the County Women's Land Army Organisation. During such times the volunteer will not pay unemployment contributions, nor will she be able to claim unemployment benefit or assistance.

The National Health Insurance cards will not be stamped during the maintenance period, but they will be franked when presented at the Ministry of Labour local office.

Acts of Bravery during Air Raids

Many a member of the Women's Land Army has been particularly brave by carrying on with her work during air raids and during machine-gunning by enemy planes. Volunteers are, of course, entitled to awards and commendations for bravery in the same way as A.R.P. workers and fire-fighters.

Resignations

A volunteer will only resign for health or urgent private reasons, and on doing so she must hand in her uniform, and, if in a position to do so, she should refund the cost of her training and equipment.

Resignations, naturally, are not welcome, for it is expected that girls who take up this vital and very important work of feeding the nation will not resign.

Starting Work

When a volunteer has been chosen to start work on a particular farm she receives the form which appears on page 62.

Accompanying this form will be a railway voucher; for further instructions in regard to travelling, payment of bus fares, advance luggage, etc., see page 79.

The volunteer should note the name of the farmer, the address of the farm and the address where she is going to lodge. She should be quite sure about the amount of her weekly wage, the amount she is going to pay each week for board and lodging and the sum to which she is entitled for overtime work. If she is in any doubt she should see her local representative immediately on arrival.

She should know the address of the County Secretary of the Women's Land Army of the county in which she is going to work, so that she can appeal to her in case of any difficulty. She should take with her her National Health Insurance card, her medical card, Unemployment Insurance card, identity card and her ration book. She should have her name entered on the panel of a nearby doctor on arrival, and she can readily find the address of the nearest Employment Exchange.

TYPE OF WORK AVAILABLE

Timber Measurers

A good education is needed for this work, and a short Government training of two or three weeks is

WOMEN'S LAND ARMY COUNTY COMMITTEE

Address *County Hall*

Lambford

62

Dear Madam,

W.L.A. No. 29382

It has been arranged for you to start work at *Blossoms Farm*, *Darley Whimple* on *Tuesday 3rd April*. Your nearest station is *Cobley Junc.* Your starting wage will be 32/- per week and living accommodation will be provided for you at *Mrs. Roseface*, *Laburnum Cottage, Darley Whimple*, at a weekly charge of

16/-. On receipt of this letter, please write without delay to *Mr. Colewin, the farmer,* saying what time you will arrive. In case of any personal difficulty apply to *the local representative, Mrs. De Laveland, Cockham Grange, Ock Whimple.*

Yours faithfully,

Caroline Workard
County Secretary.

A RAILWAY VOUCHER ACCOMPANIES THIS.

E

given at the Forestry Commissions Training Centre in the Forest of Dean before employment. During this period volunteers receive free board and lodging plus a personal allowance of 10s. per week.

At the end of their course of training, volunteers are placed in employment in couples in a forest or saw-mill at a starting wage of 45s. per week. Out of this the volunteers have to pay for their billets. The hours of work are from 7 a.m. to 4.30 p.m., with a half day off on Saturdays. Overtime must be worked if and when required.

The work includes dealing with the commoner home-grown trees and principal timbers, the measurement of sawn timber, the stacking of boards and planks for seasoning, and the care of tools. Practical work includes the measuring and cross-cutting of poles for props, the stripping of branches and bark and the supervision of waggon-loading.

Forestry Work

For this type of work volunteers receive no preliminary training, but go into immediate employment at a wage based on the existing agricultural wage rate for women in the county where they are working. This is never less than 32s. per

1. Land Girl ploughing the South Downs.

2. Land Girl operating a 22-ton military bulldozer in the first stage of clearing land of trees for agriculture.

3. Preparing ground for tomatoes in a greenhouse in the market-gardening country near Evesham.

4. Land Girl posing for the camera in full official kit.

LOCAL REPRESENTATIVE'S REPORT

County.................... Date of visit...........................194...

1. Name of Volunteer.....................................W.L.A. No.........

2. Billet Address..

3. Name of employer...

4. Is employer satisfied ?............   5. Is volunteer satisfied ?...........

6. Are billets satisfactory ?............   7. Is volunteer on local doctor's

panel ?...............

8. Is volunteer member of an approved society ?..........................

9. Are wages and overtime correctly paid ?...............................

10. If overtime is worked regularly, what are the average hours in the

working week ?.............................

11. How much time off is given each week ?................................

12. What arrangements are made for other leave ?..........................

13. Does volunteer take/see the *Land-Girl* ?..................................
    (*If subscription due, please collect and forward to county office*)

14. What arrangements have been made for recreation ?.................

....

15. General Remarks:—

....
Signature

NOTE.—Comments on uniform should not be made on this form.

5. Report form used to assess the progress of Land Girls.

6. & 7. Treading the silo. One stage in the making of ensilage, a method of preserving green fodder.

The Land Army Song. *Words and music both by Land-girls*

BACK TO THE LAND

Words by
P. ADKINS, W.L.A. 28299 & J. MONCRIEFF

Music by
E. K. LORING, W.L.A. 2053

1

Back to the Land, we must all lend a hand,
To the farms and the fields we must go.
There's a job to be done,
Though we can't fire a gun
We can still do our bit with the hoe.
When your muscles are strong
You will soon get along,
And you'll think that a country life's grand.
We're all needed now,
We must all speed the plough,
So come with us—Back to the Land.

2

Back to the Land, with its clay and its sand,
Its granite and gravel and grit,
You grow barley and wheat
And potatoes to eat
To make sure that the nation keeps fit.
Remember the rest
Are all doing their best,
To achieve the results they have planned
We will tell you once more
You can help win the war
If you come with us—Back to the Land.

Single copies 1d. each, 2d. post free, or 12 for 1s., post free, can be obtained from the Editor, "The Land Girl," Balcombe Place, Balcombe, Hayward's Heath, Sussex

8. Music and lyrics to *Back to the Land*, the Land Army song.

9. Land Girl laying hedges.

10, 11, 12, & 13.
Harvest time.

14. & 15. Land Girls caring for livestock.

16. & 17. Land Girls caring for livestock.

18. Digging ditches.

19, 20, 21, 22 & 23. The Land Army Timber Corps at work.

24. Picking apples.

week. The work includes the lopping and chopping off of timber for pit-props and the planting of young trees.

Milk-round

A certain number of volunteers are employed by producer-retailers on milk-rounds. The work consists of looking after horses, going out early on dark mornings, selling the milk, keeping the books, collecting the bottles and cheering up the house-wives! In addition, there is a certain amount of work to be done in the dairy or with the cows themselves.

Fruit-growing

Here, during the winter, the volunteer may by carrying out the necessary cultivations between the trees, either by baby tractor, by horse or by hand. There will be the pruning and spraying to do. Spraying is not always very pleasant!

In the spring there will be the spring spraying and cultivations. This will be quickly followed be fruit-thinning and summer pruning. Then there will be the soft-fruit picking and marketing, followed by the picking of the plums, and then the pears and apples. In the early winter there will always be a certain amount of apple- and pear-packing to do, sorting and grading and the like.

Market Gardening

Here a girl will concentrate on helping to grow vegetables for market. There is the preparation of the ground, either by hand or by mechanical ploughing, followed by harrowing and disc-harrowing, rolling and so on. There will be the preparation of the seed-beds, the drawing out of the drills and the sowing of the seeds. There will be the putting out of plants of all kinds, and then the interminable hoeing along the rows, so as to keep the crops free from weeds and provide a dust-mulch. There may also be the dusting and spraying of the plants, to keep down pests and diseases.

As the vegetables turn in, there is, of course, the harvesting, packing and sending of them to market, or selling of them locally, as the case may be.

There is always a lot of work in the summer: picking peas and beans, pulling carrots, pulling turnips, picking spinach, and so on.

As the winter approaches, the root crops will have to be got up and put into burys, clamps or hales, as they are called in various parts of the country. There may be frames to look after, or crops to grow under continuous cloches. There will be land to plough and leave rough for the winter frosts to act on it. There will be manure to get on to the ground and to spread, lime to apply, and potatoes to put into trays in the chitting-houses.

Glasshouse Work

The Women's Land Army volunteer who is put to work in glasshouses will have to deal entirely with the growing of food-crops. In the summer it will probably be tomatoes and cucumbers; in the spring lettuces, carrots, spinach and radishes; in May and June it might be French beans or runner beans. Some glasshouse growers have a crop of mushrooms during the winter, others force rhubarb or seakale; some specialise in mustard and cress, while others go in for early marrows, climbing up the purling-posts, in addition to any other crops they may grow.

It is very hot working under glass in the summer, particularly among cucumbers, but it is very pleasant work in the winter.

Dairy-farming

Here the work will, of course, be mainly concerned with cows and calves. There will be the rearing of the calves, the looking after the young heifers, the feeding of the bull, and the general care, feeding, cleaning and maintenance of the herd of milking cows.

There will be the milking to be done, usually very early in the morning, either by hand or machine, and the cooling of the milk. Perhaps the bottling of it, and the despatching of it to some centre, or perhaps the taking of it from house to house. It may be made into cheese; a certain amount of butter may also be produced, so there may be work in the dairy as well as in the cow-shed and out in the field.

The Poultry Farm

Girls who work on poultry farms are, of course, concerned with the care of hens, chickens, ducks, geese and perhaps turkeys. There is the regular feeding and watering twice a day. There is the cleaning of the dropping-boards and the general cleansing of the houses; the eggs have to be gathered and perhaps recorded. There may be certain types to fatten for market, and there will be birds to pluck and prepare for table.

There will be the incubating to do, and the fluffy little chicks to look after in their hovers. There may be the rearing of ducklings, or baby turkeys under broody hens. The volunteer must be prepared to treat hens which are suffering from common ailments, and may have, in addition, to prune and spray any fruit trees which are growing in the poultry-run.

Tractor-drivers

It is not only necessary to know how to steer and start a tractor: there is always the problem of driving a tractor backwards, especially with some implement attached.

Any implement attached to a tractor causes a problem, for the position and method of attachment affect the steering. Correct methods of attachment must be learned. Ploughing has to be done correctly, so that the manure is completely covered and that all the furrows are straight and of uniform depth and width. In addition to ploughing, the tractor-driver must have a knowledge of the use of harrows, cultivators, rollers, drills, reapers and binders, combine harvesters and so on.

The tractor must be kept in good condition. The volunteer is not expected to be a first-class mechanic, but she should study the makers' handbook, look over the nuts and bolts regularly, attend to lubrication, water and oil levels, and be able to supply clean fuel. Oil-changing will have to be carried out at specified times.

Sheep-farming

It is not often that a girl will be placed on a farm devoted entirely to sheep, but she may be concerned with shepherding. In this case, of course, the work entails the feeding of the sheep, the pasturing of them and driving them about from place to place. A lot of care has to be taken of them at lambing time.

Sheep, like other animals, have their troubles. They get foot-rot, for instance, and their hoofs have to be cut away and treated. They may have to be dosed with medicine. There will be tails to be cut, shearing to be done and a certain amount of carting and the despatching of the animals to market.

The General Farm

By far the greater number of volunteers are employed on general farms, where the work is very varied indeed.   If it is mainly an arable farm, it will produce wheat, barley, oats, beans, potatoes, etc.   There will therefore be the land to prepare, the potatoes to plant, etc.   There will also be harrowing and rolling to be done, " thistle-dodging ", earthing-up the potatoes, spraying them and the general care of the crops.   There may be fruit to pick in the summer; there will be hay to make and cart.

In the summer, too, there will be the corn to cut, the sheaves to deal with, the stacking to be done, horses to stable and groom, the stubble to rake. Later there will be the potatoes to pick up and bag, together with the marketing or clamping.

There may be cows to look after, calves to feed, pigs to feed and clean, and perhaps poultry and rabbits to look after.   In the winter there will be the hedging and ditching, the manure-carting, the threshing and chaff-cutting, the fence repairs, the barbed-wire work, the dressing of the barley, wheats and oats.   In fact, the jobs on the general farm never end.

CHAPTER VII

WELFARE

The Local Representative—Combined rallies—News letters
—*The Land Girl* Magazine—The County Library.

THE general welfare of members of the Women's Land Army is supervised in each county by the County Secretary. Besides the assistance of a County Committee, she has the help of voluntary workers familiar with their respective districts. These undertake to keep in touch with the Women's Land Army volunteers working within their own district.

The volunteer is not just put to work on a farm or market-garden and then forgotten by County Headquarters. Regular reports are made on her well-being, at any rate for the first few months, and the volunteer can always write in to her County Headquarters if she is in any difficulty.

The Local Representative

The Local Representative of the Women's Land Army is really responsible for the general welfare of the girls in her district. She will go and visit the farmer and make contact with him. Having done this, she will see the landlady of the billet where the girl is living and find out if everything is all right there. She will probably ask the girl up to tea and chat over things with her. She will arrange to put her in touch with the local Women's Institute, with the Girls' Friendly Society, with the Y.W.C.A. or with any clubs for girls there may be in the district.

If the girl is a member of the Church of England, she will put her in touch with the local vicar, or, if a nonconformist, with a minister of a suitable church near by.

She will, in fact, try to make her as happy as possible in her new surroundings. She will explain to her the amenities of the village or country town. She will tell her about postal facilities, and any local or country libraries there may be. She will inform her as to the nearest doctor and advise her about chemists, shops and shopping. She will tell her about the local Employment Exchange, and help her with difficulties over ration cards and rationing.

She will, of course, obtain the billets for the girl and see that these are suitable. Where there is no bathroom in the cottage, she will try to arrange for friends near by to offer the use of their bathroom at stated times each week.

The Local Representative, it will be seen, acts in a similar capacity to the Women's Land Army as the Military Welfare Officer does for the troops. She tries to make the volunteer's spare time as happy as possible, and she helps her with her difficulties and problems.

The County Library

In every county there is a County Library, and a County Librarian with assistants to look after it. Books are available free of charge for all residents in the county. The usual rule is for the county to pay the postage one way and for the recipient to pay the postage back.

The County Library is there for all Women's Land Army volunteers to make use of, and not only has all types of fiction, but offers a complete range of agricultural and horticultural books, which will be of great help to the volunteer who is keen on studying her newly found profession.

In many cases there will be a local branch of the County Library in the village, and the Land Girl will be able to change her books with the voluntary local librarian and to ask her to obtain the books she requires. Sometimes this library is run in connection with the school, and sometimes in connection with the village hall.

Occasional Classes

Where there are a number of volunteers in a town, village or district, the County Secretary or the Local Representative may be able to arrange for a short series of lectures to be given by the County Council Advisers or by members of the County War Agricultural Executive staff. These lectures would deal with the aspect of agriculture or horticulture in which the girls were most interested. In a market-gardening district it would probably be vegetable-growing, in a dairying county milk production, and so on.

These classes or lectures may consist of a series of three or six, or it may only be possible to run one every now and then. In addition, in the summer time it should be possible to arrange for demonstrations in the open air of definite farming operations or on the control of pests and diseases. Some County Committees arrange tests and competitions in milking, ploughing, hedging and ditching, etc., for their volunteers, and these are judged by local farmers.

Combined Rallies

In many counties occasional combined rallies are held on a Saturday afternoon or on such days and at such times as best suit the farmers of the locality. All volunteers within easy distance are invited. Food is somehow provided, and a good time is had by all. It may be possible for the County Chairman to invite the girls to her own house in the summer and take them round the garden, or there may be a big farmer near by who is willing to take the girls over and explain his way of doing things.

It is sometimes possible to arrange for Land Girls to visit a Research Station, or the farm and grounds of a college or Farm Institute. In Lincolnshire and Norfolk they might be taken to see a sugar-beet factory in full work.

It must not be thought that the Land Girl is constantly going about on trips, but it does make for "esprit de corps," and it does give a girl a feeling of being a member of an important army,

if she can from time to time meet others and
learn more of the profession in which she is
employed.

Parties!

There is no reason at all why little parties should
not be arranged for a few girls in any town or village.
Sometimes the girls themselves arrange these, and
perhaps pay a visit to the local cinema together, or
meet for a game of cards or a good gossip round the
fire. The Land Army volunteer must be prepared
to help with her own welfare, and she can do much
to make her own life happy if she tries to make
others happy too.

The News Letter

Several counties now send out News Letters to
their volunteers. In this way the girls are kept in
touch with the other girls working in the same
county, and all local news as well as national news
reaches them in a personal manner from the County
Secretary.

The volunteers are encouraged to send their news
from time to time to be published in the News Letter,
and personal notes prove a very interesting feature,

and help friends in the same Army to keep in touch with one another.

" *The Land Girl* " *Magazine*

Every month there is published an excellent magazine called *The Land Girl.* In it news appears from every county, and, in addition, dealing with tractor-driving, dairying, horticulture, etc., as well as the personal experiences of the volunteers, competitions and official news.

The magazine is priced at 3*d.* per copy, or 3*s.* a year post free. Cash must be sent with order.

All communications should be addressed to the Editor, *The Land Girl* Magazine, Balcombe Place, Balcombe, Hayward's Heath, Sussex.

Land Army Song

At parties and rallies the Land Army Song is usually sung. It is easy to learn, cheerful to sing and helps to create the right spirit. Copies are obtainable from the Editor of *The Land Girl* Magazine for 1*d.* each or 2*d.* post free.

CHAPTER VIII

JOURNEYS AND HOLIDAYS

Types of Journeys for which Regular Force Volunteers Fares are Payable from Women's Land Army Funds.

1. Journey of a trainee to her place of training.

2. Journey of a trainee from her place of training to her first place of employment (except in the case of a timber measurer,when the fare is paid by the Forestry Commission), or home, if employment is not immediately available for her at the end of her training course, or if her training is interrupted through no fault of her own.

3. Journey of a volunteer from her home to her first place of employment—unless she leaves her county of enrolment to take up first employment in another county on her own initiative, and not because the County Secretary of the employing county has found it necessary to apply for a worker either to Women's Land Army Headquarters or to

the County Secretary of the enrolling county. In this case the volunteer will be regarded as having changed her county of residence at her own desire, and is only entitled to claim her fare within the employing county, and not from her county of first enrolment.

4. Journey of a volunteer direct from one Land Army job to another.

5. Journey of a volunteer, who is to be maintained by the county during temporary unemployment, from her job to any new billet or hostel where she is to be maintained, and the journey from her billet or hostel to the next job.

6. Journey of an unemployed volunteer from her Land Army job to her home if the county decides not to maintain her during her temporary unemployment; also the journey from her home to her next Land Army job.

7. Journeys of an *enrolled* volunteer, whom it is necessary to interview, from her billet to the county office or to the house of the district representative if the cost of this journey is equal to or less than that of a visit to the volunteer at her billet or farm.

8. Journey to her home in another county of a volunteer who has lost her Land Army job and

has been discharged from the Women's Land Army if she is destitute, and would become a burden on the resources of the locality.

9. Return from place of employment to home in England or Wales of a volunteer who has, since the outbreak of war, completed six months' Women's Land Army service on the land at least 20 miles from her home, and whose service is regarded as satisfactory by the County Office. In the case of a volunteer whose home is in Scotland or Ireland, the cost of the part of her journey to the Border or to the port of embarkation may be met.

N.B.—Daily journeys from home to work or training may not be paid for out of Women's Land Army funds.

Issue of Travelling Warrants to Cover Third-class Rail Fares

Special travelling warrants are available for issue by County Secretaries to cover third-class single rail fares in the case of types of Women's Land Army travel Nos. 1 to 8 above. Other special travelling warrants are available for issue by County Secretaries to cover third-class *return* rail fares in the case of type 9 above of Women's Land Army travel.

Warrants for journeys *from* Training Centres will naturally be issued by the Head of the Training Centre, instead of by the County Secretaries.

Travelling Expenses of Trainees

A travelling warrant will be issued to each trainee for the third-class rail fare for her journey from her home to her place of training.

At the end of training, travelling warrants will be issued to trainees who have trained on a farm by the office of the county in which the training took place and to trainees who have trained at a Training Centre by the Head of that Training Centre.

In the case of farm trainees, claims for bus fares and cost of sending luggage in advance will usually be paid by the County Office.

In the case of trainees trained at Training Centres, the claims for bus fares, cost of sending luggage in advance, etc., will be met by the Head of the Training Centre on arrival. In the same way, when the volunteer leaves the Training Centre at the end of her course, the Head will meet her claims for bus fares and for sending luggage in advance away from the Centre, though any bus fares or cost of luggage which have to be paid at the other end of the journey will be dealt with by the County Office.

Volunteers whose training is interrupted through no fault of their own and who have to be sent home will have travelling warrants issued to them.

Timber Measurers

Travelling warrants will be issued by the authorities at the Forestry School, Park End, to timber measurers leaving the school for employment after training.

Incidental expenses will be refunded to timber measurers by the Divisional Officers of the Forestry Commission on receipt of a claim on form A/cs. GEN.8, copies of which will be obtained from the Forestry School. These claims *will not* be paid out of Women's Land Army funds.

Journeys undertaken by a timber measurer when proceeding from one job to another will be paid for by the Forestry Commission as her employer.

Holiday Rail Facilities

As has already been stated, a Women's Land Army Volunteer is entitled to one free *return* journey voucher for every six months satisfactorily completed Land Army service, if she is at least 20 miles from home.

This is limited to a journey to a home in England or Wales, or, in the case of a volunteer whose home is in Scotland or Ireland, to a journey to the Border or port of embarkation.

After her leave the volunteer is of course expected to return to her Land Army employment.

" *Title* " *to Holidays*

The railway facility offered does not necessarily mean that a volunteer will be able to obtain a holiday in which to visit her home, or that she will be able to obtain it exactly when she would like.

Her title to a holiday naturally depends on the terms of her employment and of any order of the County Agricultural Wages Board, which may provide for holidays with pay.

The free journey may therefore be undertaken by the volunteer at any time after the completion of six months' Land Army service, the *actual date* of the journey being arranged by the volunteer *with her employer* to suit their mutual convenience. It is sometimes necessary for the journey to be temporarily deferred owing to the needs of the farmer.

CHAPTER IX

LIST OF CHAIRMEN AND COUNTY SECRETARIES

Giving all Addresses and Telephone Numbers

County.	Chairman.	Secretary.
BEDFORDSHIRE	Mrs. J. A. Whitchurch, Great Barford House, Bedford.	Mrs. Heydeman, 2, St. Paul's Square, Bedford. *Tel*. Bedford 3201.
BERKSHIRE	Mrs. Howard Palmer, Heathlands, Wokingham, Berks. *Tel*. Wokingham 3.	Mrs. Norman May, 7, Abbots Walk, The Forbury, Reading. *Tel*. Reading 60194.
BUCKINGHAMSHIRE	Lady Hermione Cobbold, Studdridge Farm, Stokenchurch, High Wycombe, Bucks. *Tel*. Radnage 103.	Miss M. J. Parry, 6, St. Mary's Street, High Wycombe. *Tel*. High Wycombe 1406.
CAMBRIDGESHIRE	*See under* HUNTINGDONSHIRE.	
CAMBRIDGESHIRE, ISLE OF ELY	*See under* HUNTINGDONSHIRE.	
CHESHIRE	Mrs. Ernest Johnson, M.B.E., J.P., Ashton Hayes, Chester. *Tel*. Kelsall 209.	Miss E. L. Manley, Odeon Building, Northgate Street, Chester. *Tel*. Chester 447.
CORNWALL	Mrs. C. Williams, Caerhays Castle, Gorran. *Tel*. Veryan 250.	Mrs. Clifford Smith, W.L.A. Office, 2, Farley Terrace, Truro. *Tel*. Truro 2958.

County.	Chairman.	Secretary.
CUMBERLAND and WESTMORLAND	Mrs. MacInnes, Rose Bank, Penrith, Cumberland. *Tel.* Pooley Bridge 58. Miss C. M. Elmslie, Brathay How, Ambleside, Westmorland. *Tel.* Ambleside 89.	Miss M. A. Soulsby, Women's Land Army, 11, Crown Square, Penrith, Cumberland. *Tel.* Penrith 265.
DERBYSHIRE	Her Grace The Duchess of Devonshire, Churchdale Hall, Ashford, Bakewell, Derbyshire. *Tel.* Great Longstone 9.	Miss E. Fryer, Imperial Chambers, Dale Road, Matlock, Derbyshire. *Tel.* Matlock 522.
DEVONSHIRE	The Countess Fortescue, Castle Hill, Barnstaple, Devonshire. *Tel.* Filleigh 227.	Miss H. Medley-Costin, 59, High Street, Exeter, Devonshire. *Tel.* Exeter 54866.
DORSET	Miss W. Marsden, O.B.E., The Greaves, Prince of Wales Road, Dorchester. *Tel.* Dorchester 103.	Mrs. M. C. Heenan, 28a, High East Street, Dorchester. *Tel.* Dorchester 787.
DURHAM	Mrs. Lloyd Pease, Hurworth Moor, Darlington, Co. Durham. *Tel.* Darlington 2179.	Miss M. Stapleton, Eggleshope House, Egglestone, Co. Durham. *Tel.* Cotherstone 35.
ESSEX	Miss Olive Tritton, Brent Hall, Finchingfield, Braintree, Essex. *Tel.* Great Bardfield 26.	Mrs. R. E. Solly Flood, W.L.A. County Office, Institute of Agriculture, Writtle, nr. Chelmsford. *Tel.* Writtle 221.
GLOUCESTERSHIRE	Mrs. W. S. Morrison, The Manor House, Withington, Cheltenham, Glos. *Tel.* Withington (Cheltenham) 35.	The Hon. Mrs. W. R. S. Bathurst, Winterbourne Park, Bristol, Glos. *Tel.* Winterbourne 71.

County.	Chairman.	Secretary.
HAMPSHIRE	Mrs. Chute, The Vyne, Basingstoke, Hants. *Tel.* Bramley Green 227.	Mrs. E. M. Cherrington, The Castle, Winchester, Hants. *Tel.* Winchester 1000, Ext. 59–62.
HEREFORDSHIRE	Mrs. E. Barnardiston, O.B.E., Bernithan Court, Ross-on-Wye, Herefordshire. *Tel.* Llangarron 24.	Miss Hope Hannyngton, 131, St. Owen Street, Hereford. *Tel.* Hereford 3569.
HERTFORDSHIRE	Mrs. E. Martin Smith, Lane House, Kings Walden, Hitchin, Herts. *Tel.* Offley 49.	Miss C. Beck, Women's Land Army, County Hall, Hertford. *Tel.* Hertford 3131. *Ext.* 286.
HUNTINGDONSHIRE, CAMBRIDGESHIRE and ISLE OF ELY	Lady Gray, Gog Magog Hills, Babraham, Cambs. *Tel.* Cambridge 87564.	Mrs. Warde, Women's Land Army, Lawrence Court, Huntingdon. *Tel.* Huntingdon 126.
ISLE OF WIGHT	Lady Baring, Nubia House, Cowes, Isle of Wight. *Tel.* Cowes 27.	Miss A. M. Hume, The Mount, Tetland Bay, Isle of Wight. *Tel.* Freshwater 9.
KENT—EAST	The Lady Cornwallis, " Plovers," Horsmonden, Kent. *Tel.* Horsmonden 16.	Miss M. Smythe, M.B.E., Winchelsea House, Longport Street, Canterbury, Kent. *Tel.* Canterbury 4377.
KENT—WEST	The Lady Cornwallis, " Plovers," Horsmonden, Kent. *Tel.* Horsmonden 16. *Vice-chairman:* Mrs. F. J. Heron-Maxwell, Great Comp, Borough Green, Kent. *Tel.* Borough Green 409.	Miss V. M. M. Cox, Great Comp, Borough Green, Kent. *Tel.* Borough Green 409.

County.	Chairman.	Secretary.
LANCASHIRE	Lady Worsley-Taylor, J.P., Townhead, nr. Clitheroe, Lancs. *Tel.* Clitheroe 89.	Mrs. Robertson, Women's Land Army, County Offices, Preston, Lancs. *Tel.* Preston 4868, Ext Man. 13.
LEICESTERSHIRE and RUTLAND	The Hon. Lady Martin, J.P., The Brand, Loughborough, Leics. *Tel.* Woodhouse-Eaves 269. Miss A. S. Brocklebank, O.B.E., J.P., Wing Grange, Oakham, Rutland. *Tel.* Manton 4.	Miss D. M. Elliot, 132, Regent Road, Leicester. *Tel.* Leicester 21125.
LINCOLNSHIRE, HOLLAND and KESTEVEN	The Hon. Mrs. Hoos, Frieston House, Caythorpe, Grantham. *Tel.* Fulbeck 288.	Mrs. Hill, 43, Boston Road, Sleaford, Lincs. *Tel.* Sleaford 446.
LINCOLNSHIRE, LINDSEY	Mrs. M. Wintringham, J.P., White Cottage, Tealby, Lincs. *Tel.* Tealby 212.	Miss I. M. S. Rowley, 8, St. Peter-at-Arches, Silver Street, Lincoln. *Tel.* Lincoln 665.
MIDDLESEX and LONDON	Mrs. E. Beale, Green Doors, Stanwell Moor, nr. Staines, Middlesex. *Tel.* Colnbrook 63.	Mrs. J. H. S. Sykes, 284. High Street, Uxbridge, *Tel.* Uxbridge 222.
MONMOUTHSHIRE	Lady Mather-Jackson, C.B.E., St. Mary's Hill, Abergavenny, Mon. *Tel.* Nantyderry 24.	Miss C. E. E. Hopkin, Lindisfarne, Monmouth Road, Abergavenny, Mon. *Tel.* Abergavenny 411.
NORFOLK	The Dowager Lady Suffield, J.P., Harbord House, Cromer, Norfolk. *Tel.* Cromer 2488.	Miss Iris Tillett, 3, Castle Street, Norwich, Norfolk. *Tel.* Norwich 1280.
NORTHAMPTON-SHIRE	The Countess Spencer, Althorp, Northants. *Tel.* East Haddon 200.	Mrs. F. J. Simpson, 6, Market Square, Higham Ferrers, Northants. *Tel.* Rushden 659.

County.	Chairman.	Secretary.
NORTHUMBERLAND	The Countess Grey, C.B.E., Howick, Alnwick, Northumberland. *Tel.* Longhoughton 21.	Mrs. F. C. Clement, Linnel Dene, Hexham, Northumberland. *Tel.* Hexham 351.
NOTTINGHAMSHIRE	The Lady Sibell Argles, White Lodge, Thoresby Park, Ollerton, Notts. *Tel.* Edwinstowe 28.	Miss N. Moore, The Women's Land Army Office, The Kennels, Thoresby Park, Ollerton, Notts. *Tel.* Edwinstowe 98.
OXFORDSHIRE	Miss G. M. Ashhurst, Waterstock, Wheatley, S.O., Oxfordshire. *Tel.* Ickford 21.	Miss C. Hole, Agricultural Economics Institute, Parks Road, Oxford. *Tel.* Oxford 47548.
RUTLAND	*See under* LEICESTERSHIRE.	
SHROPSHIRE	The Viscountess Boyne, C.B.E., Burwarton House, Bridgnorth, Shropshire. *Vice-Chairman :* Mrs. Donaldson-Hudson, Cheswardine, Market Drayton, Shropshire.	Mrs. J. A. Preston, Women's Land Army Office, County Buildings, Shrewsbury, Salop. *Tel.* Shrewsbury 3031, Ext. 79.
SOMERSET	Lady Langman, North Cadbury Court, Yeovil, Somerset. *Tel.* North Cadbury 202.	Miss B. Spencer, B.A., 30, Bridge Street, Taunton, Somerset. *Tel.* Taunton 2885.
STAFFORDSHIRE	Miss R. M. Harrison, O.B.E., M.F.H., Maer Hall, Newcastle, Staffs. *Tel.* Whitmore 207.	Mrs. Frith, Swynnerton Rectory, Stone, Staffs. *Tel.* Swynnerton 32 or Stafford 838.
SUFFOLK—EAST	The Lady Cranworth, Grundisburgh Hall, Woodbridge, Suffolk. *Tel.* Grundisburgh 202.	Mrs. Sunderland Taylor, Women's Land Army Office, County Hall, Ipswich, Suffolk. *Tel.* Ipswich 2874.

County.	Chairman.	Secretary.
SUFFOLK—WEST	Lady Briscoe, Lakenheath Hall, Suffolk. *Tel.* Lakenheath 2.	Mrs. Lindsay Scott, Women's Land Army Office, Crescent House, Angel Hill, Bury St. Edmunds, Suffolk. *Tel.* Bury St. Edmunds 551.
SURREY	The Hon. Mrs. E. F. Bray, Vachery, Shere, Surrey.	Miss S. Sharp, Education Office, Park Street, Guildford, Surrey. *Tel.* Guildford 3779.
SUSSEX—EAST	The Countess De La Warr, Fishers Gate, Withyham, Sussex. *Tel.* Hartfield 46.	Mrs. R. Lowman, Cockhaise, Lindfield, Sussex. *Hel.* Lindfield 113.
SUSSEX—WEST	The Hon. Mrs. Burrell, Church Farm North, Shipley, Horsham, Sussex. *Tel.* Coolham 261.	Miss Forbes Adam, 8, Worthing Road, Horsham, Sussex. *Tel.* Horsham 821.
WARWICKSHIRE	Mrs. J. Fielden, O.B.E., Kineton House, Warwicks. *Tel.* Kineton 16.	Miss M. E. Colwell, 24, Old Square, Warwicks. *Tel.* Warwick 491.
WESTMORLAND	*See under* CUMBERLAND	
WILTSHIRE	The Hon. Mrs. Methuen, Ivy House, Corsham, Wilts.	The Lady Katharine McNeil, Nonsuch, Bromham, Chippenham, Wilts. *Tel.* Bromham 34.
WORCESTERSHIRE	Mrs. T. Lea, M.A., J.P., Coneybury, Bayton, Kidderminster, Worcs. *Tel.* Clows Top 23.	Mrs. G. T. Coombs, 5, Foregate Street, Worcester. *Tel.* Worcester 2402.
YORKSHIRE—EAST RIDING	Mrs. Carver, Ryland Hill, South Cave, Brough. *Tel.* Brough 21.	Miss S. Grotrian, Roos House, Roos, E. Yorkshire. *Tel.* Burton Pidsea 50.

County.	Chairman.	Secretary.
YORKSHIRE— NORTH RIDING	Lady (Guy) Graham, Norton Conyers, Melmerby, Ripon, Yorks. *Tel.* Melmerby 3.	Miss W. Jacob Smith, Somerley, Knaresborough, Yorks. *Tel.* Knaresborough 3116.
YORKSHIRE—WEST RIDING	The Lady Bingley, Bramham Park, Boston Spa, Yorks. *Tel.* Boston Spa 14.	Miss G. Harrison, Walcot, Alexandra Road, Harrogate, Yorks. *Tel.* Harrogate 5434.

Wales

County.	Chairman.	Secretary.
NORTH WALES AREA Anglesey Caernarvonshire Merionethshire Montgomeryshire	Miss E. Griffith, Bryn, Nr. Caernarvon.	Mrs. Edmunds Edwards, B.A., National Provincial Bank Chambers, Bangor, Caernarvonshire. *Tel.* Bangor 391.
SOUTH WALES AREA Glamorganshire Brecon & Radnor Cardiganshire Carmarthenshire Pembrokeshire	Miss G. Lloyd Price, B.A., J.P., Talardd, Maesy Crugian, Carmarthen- *Tel.* Llanybyther 232.	Miss D. E. Bishop, Colonial Buildings, Little Water Street, Carmarthen. *Tel.* Carmarthen 7286.
DENBIGHSHIRE	Mrs. J. C. Wynne Finch, Voelas, Bettws-y-Coed, Caernarvonshire. *Tel.* Pontrevoelas 6.	Miss B. Blew, Hafod, Trefnant, nr. Denbigh, Denbighshire. *Tel.* Trefnant 317.
FLINTSHIRE	Miss M. Bibby, Fachwen, St. Asaph, North Wales.	Mrs. Peyton (Hon. Sec.), Hafod, Mold, Flintshire. *Tel.* Mold 65.

CHAPTER X

MAKING THE MOST OF THE COUNTRY

THE town girl does not often find it easy to live in
the country.   She naturally misses all the amenities
that she is used to.   She cannot pop in to the local
cinema when she feels inclined.   She cannot even
go round to the local fish-and-chip shop or to a
snack bar if she wants a quick meal in the evening.
She is not able to stroll down the High Street and
have a look at the shops and see the latest fashions,
and there are not, of course, the number of men
about to go to dances with at the local Palais de
Dance.

Some townspeople are apt to look upon all
country folk as country bumpkins.   They have an
idea that it is only the town folk who know any-
thing, and because people in the country are not so
slick, or are not so well dressed, or perhaps are not
up to the latest fashion, they are apt to be labelled
as old-fashioned, and rather a back number.

Actually, country folk usually know far more

than those who are bred and born in towns and cities. They may not know all the names of the film stars and the pictures in which they have appeared, but they do know the names of the birds and their habits. They are able to tell whether it is going to be wet or fine the next day. They know which herbs are useful and all about the ways of wild animals. They have a different kind of knowledge, that is all.

The Land Army volunteer, therefore, who is going to work on a farm and live in a village must be prepared to see the " other fellow's " point of view. She will never be a success if she goes into her new surroundings determined to show them a thing or two. She will only be stared at if she wears her very latest Bond Street creation at the local social or "hop." She will be considered rude if she is continually saying, " Fancy you not knowing that ", or is constantly boasting of her doings in the town.

It does need a little effort at first to fit in with new surroundings. It is always necessary to consider the farmer and his family; to consider the billeter, and to remember to help in the little things, and to lend a hand sometimes without being asked.

There are so many obvious things which get forgotten. The volunteer should always be punctual in her hours; she should not smoke about the place, especially in farm buildings; she should shut gates behind her; she should put tools back properly, so that the next person who wants them can find them; she should never leave a job half done just because she finds it difficult.

A farmer is not made in a month, and, after training, some girls are inclined to try to teach the farmer his business, often with unfortunate results. So if a volunteer has been taught a method different from the farmer's, she should always ask his permission before making the change. Farmers have no time to bother with fussy volunteers. They expect girls who have offered to do the work to carry it out without complaint.

Trying it Out

A volunteer who enrols to " see if she likes it " is a liability, not an asset. However patriotic she may feel, she does not help her country by enrolling in the Land Army unless she is certain she can stay the course.

It is quite a good plan to try carrying buckets full

of water for half an hour or more at a time, and then attempting to pitch earth onto a barrow and then onto a shelf about breast high for another hour or so, to see whether she can bear the aches and pains entailed.   Farming work is not spectacular, but it does mean hard physical strain, but any girl who can endure it finds compensation in the knowledge that she is playing a very important part in National Service.

Dissatisfaction

Some farm jobs are monotonous, but they are essential to food production. The volunteer should do them thoroughly and systematically, for by putting her best into the work she will make it interesting.

If, however, she is not completely happy, or is dissatisfied in any way, she should not throw up her job hastily, or grumble to her fellow-workers. The matter should be taken to the farmer himself, the County Secretary consulted or the District Representative talked to, and in this way it is usually possible to get matters put right.

Make-up

Town girls on the whole use far more make-up

G

than country girls. The Women's Land Army volunteer should therefore be prepared to " tone down " her lips, complexions and nails considerably.

A certain amount of make-up may be used at parties and local village dances, but long nails are quite unsuited to work on a farm, especially when covered with bright crimson nail-varnish.

The volunteer will soon find that, as the other girls from the village do not use make-up, she will prefer not to use it herself, so as not to look conspicuous. She will find, too, that she will get such a healthy colour to her cheeks that rouging will not be necessary!

Lending a Hand

Be prepared to do some useful work in the village during your spare time. It may be that you can get into touch with the local representative of the W.V.S. and do some knitting. Perhaps you will be able to help by forming one of the personnel of the village First-Aid Point. You can be very useful, too, by putting your name down as one of the fire-watchers.

Some Land Army volunteers have taken on

definite voluntary jobs in the villages. At least one is organising the local branch of the County Library, and is very much liked and appreciated as a result.

Socials

Join the local Women's Institute, and go to their meetings if they are held at a convenient time. Go to any socials there may be in the village, and try to fit in naturally. Don't push yourself, and so spoil things. Take part in all such activities in a humble manner, and help to break down any prejudice there may be against women on the land. Each volunteer can do her part to ensure smooth working and to help in securing the good name of the Women's Land Army.

Maids

When living at a farm where a maid is kept, the volunteer should remember that she also is employed by the farmer, and not by herself. She should not therefore expect the maid to wait on her, nor should she give the maid extra work and extra bother.

Sticking To It

The Land Army is judged by its members. A good volunteer is a good advertisement.

Every volunteer should remember that money has been spent on her equipment and training, to make her a *a specialist* for a vital job. She should not, therefore, *ever drop out*. She must feel that *she* is feeding the nation. If she drops out, some-one may starve.

Further, wherever a recruit or a full Women's Land Army volunteer gives up, she represents a dead loss to her county, and her county cannot afford dead losses in a war like this.

There is the example to think of, too. If one volunteer gives up, it has an effect on others. Recruits coming along get to know, and so " rot " may set in.

The Land Army must have a motto—" Stick to It."

Girls who had to resign in the early days of the war for a good reason, or just to change their jobs, or even to go home, are wanted—they should, therefore, if reliable, offer their services once more, for they are certainly needed.

Training given at the Government's expense will thus *not* be wasted, nor will the experience gained be lost.

CHAPTER XI

USEFUL HINTS AND TIPS

Remedy for Roughened Hands

Put 1 ounce of olive oil and 1 ounce chopped beeswax into a jar in the oven until melted. Cool and, when easy to handle, roll into a ball. Rub lightly into the hands after washing. A little oat flour will remove greasiness.

Making Shoes Waterproof

Cut up a little beeswax and put into a jar. Cover with a little castor oil or neat's-foot oil. Stand in a warm place till wax is melted. Stir thoroughly. Allow to cool. If too thick add a little more oil.

To use, warm a little, apply with stiff brush while quite soft. Let that coat harden, warm boots slightly, and apply another coat. Neat's-foot oil alone is quite good.

To Make Gum Boots Slip on and Off Easily

Sprinkle French chalk inside the gum boots from time to time.

Making Gum Boots Last Longer

Wash them every day, removing mud, dung-oil and milk. All these have a detrimental effect on the rubber.

Saving Stockings in Gum Boots

Wear a pair of slipper socks over Land Army stockings, or cut the feet from an old pair of woollen stockings, or buy a pair of ankle socks.

Treating Wet Shoes or Boots

Stuff as tightly as possible with newspaper, then *dry slowly*. *Never* put close to a fire or on top of an oven.

Making Stockings Last Longer

The volunteers should wear the three pairs issued to them in rotation. They will thus last much longer than if one pair is kept for best and two are worn to rags. Wash in a good soap powder. Do not rub. Squeeze stockings gently and rinse in warm water. Pull to their proper shape before hanging up to dry.

FIRST AID

Bites of Animals

If these are at all serious, they should be seen by a doctor at once. Otherwise, treat as for cuts, and make sure that the bottom of the wound is thoroughly cleansed and disinfected.

Chapped Hands

After washing the hands, work in soap till all is absorbed and the hands are dry. Apply glycerine night and morning before quite drying the hands.

Chilblains

Exercise the toes and fingers whenever possible. Do *not* wear wool socks or stockings next the skin. Apply ointment consisting of 10 grains of menthol to 1 ounce of olive oil. Dress broken chilblains with gauze; keep this on with plaster.

Cracked Thumbs

Apply Zambuk, castor oil or oil of wintergreen, and cover with Elastoplast or a thumb-stall to keep clean.

Nail in Shoe

Clean and disinfect the wound thoroughly. A little gauze or cotton wool wound round a match or orange-stick and dipped in weak disinfectant can be probed to base of wound.

Root-pulling

For any work where you have to pull, the wearing of a wrist strap or a bandage over the wrist is useful.

Scratches

Clean and disinfect as for cuts, but leave exposed, unless working with manure, etc., when scratches should be covered.

Stye or Sore Eyes

Bathe in warm, *weak* salt water.

Wasp and Bee-stings, Insect-bites

Squeeze out sting if left in wound. Apply blue-bag, household ammonia, or soda.

Weight-lifting

Start to lift with legs well apart, body bent at waist, tummy-muscles braced. Wearing a belt does help support muscles for heavy lifting.

CHAPTER XII

THE PROOF OF THE PUDDING IS IN THE EATING

Farmers' Opinions—Volunteers' Opinions

1. *Mr. H. M., Cheltenham:*

"We have two permanent workers on this farm, and I take off my hat to them both. They have never yet complained, nor once hesitated to tackle any job given them to do, and are always on time in any weather."

2. *The Executive Officer, Cheshire War Agricultural Executive Committee:*

"The Women's Land Army has made good; of that there can be no question. There are indeed many labours on the land which they cannot do; but there are very many which they not only can do but are in fact already doing."

3. *A Hants. Farmer:*

"You will see from our reports on the two girls you sent us that we are more than pleased with them. If they are not exceptions, we can only say that the Women's Land Army is a great success. They are very happy in their work and in their diggings. They are both most anxious to give of their best, and they are most useful. . . ."

4. *A Hexham Farmer :*

" As you know, I was very doubtful about the wisdom of taking two girls who had had no previous experience. My fears were quite groundless. They have been quick to learn, and have worked hard at all manner of tasks—not a few of them both dirty and uncongenial. I have nothing but praise for them."

5. *An Isle of Ely, Cambs., Farmer :*

" You might like to know the kind of work which my land girl does :—

    (1) Drives away at manure-cart, etc.

    (2) Harrows in with one horse behind a drill.

    (3) Loads straw when at litter-cart.

    (4) Holds sacks when putting up corn.

    (5) When chaff-cutting pushes the straw to the feeder.

    (6) Takes off chaff when threshing.

(7) Took up quite a lot of beet, and always earned her money and a little more at £2 per acre.

(8) Takes up mangolds very well.

" So you can see that she has adapted herself to mixed farming very well after about six months, and I will say I have never heard her grumble once, and she has been out in all weathers."

6. *A Farndon, Notts., Farmer :*

" During September, 1939, I needed extra men on my farm, and being unable to get them, employed two land girls.   One was over 21 and had a science degree, and the other was 17 years old and an L.R.A.M.

" Both were keen, and most anxious to do their best.   They learnt to pitch and load a heavy second crop of seeds, and kept the men on the stacks busy until all was stacked. They drove a tractor, harrowed up twitch, which they carted and burned, had a whole week's threshing, one on the corn-stacks and the other on the straw-stacks, taking a man's place in each case, and keeping pace with the men.   They fed and cleaned out pigs and learnt to milk daily; they picked potatoes and took on four acres of beet, of which they made an excellent job, afterwards helping to load the beet into the lorry.

" I found them cheerful and willing, with never a grumble in rain or storm, always sensibly clad and happy. Girls like this cannot but help to win the war."

---

7. *A Women's Land Army Volunteer in East Sutton, Kent :*

" I have been here over a year now, and am getting more and more interested in my work, and am given more responsible jobs. . . . I am doing work which I like but would never have done but for the war. I suppose I am helping my country, but I am certainly enjoying myself too."

8. *A Women's Land Army Volunteer in Hunton, Kent :*

" I think it is about time I wrote and told you how I am getting on and how very happy I am in my job here. . . . Sheila and I only have the cows to deal with; there are 35 of them, and all dears. All the people here are extremely nice to us, and we often get invited out."

9. *A Volunteer in Soham, Cambs. :*

" I love working here. I have also learnt to milk, although I must confess I still like looking after the pigs best. It's good to see them grow so quickly. . . . I now have to work a steamer to cook potatoes for the pigs. I cook 15 cwt. a day. I manage the boiler very well. This is another job I have learnt. I also have lovely lodgings and am very happy.

10. *Women's Land Army Volunteer, Staffs. :*

" I do wish the Land Army every success, as I am so keen and happy, although for the last few days we all have gone home drenched, but still smiling."

APPENDIX

AVOIRDUPOIS WEIGHT

16 drams	=	1 ounce (oz.)
16 ounces	=	1 pound (lb.)
14 pounds	=	1 stone (st.)
28 ,,	=	1 quarter (qr.)
4 quarters or 112 pounds	=	1 hundredweight (cwt.)
20 hundredweights or 2240 pounds	=	1 ton
8 pounds	=	1 stone

(London Meat Market.)

100 pounds	=	1 cental or new cwt.

(Order in Council, 4th February, 1879.)

50 pounds	=	1 half-cental

(Order in Council, 9th October, 1903.)

LIQUID MEASURE

4 gills	= 1 pint		18 gallons	=	1 kilderkin
2 pints	= 1 quart		36 ,,	=	1 barrel
4 quarts	= 1 gallon		54 ,,	=	1 hogshead
9 gallons	= 1 firkin				

1 gallon of water weighs 10 lbs.

LONG MEASURE

7·92 inches	= 1 link	4 poles	= 1 chain
12 inches	= 1 foot	40 ,,	= 1 furlong
3 feet	= 1 yard	8 furlongs	= 1 mile
6 ,,	= 1 fathom	3 miles	= 1 league
5½ yards	= 1 pole, rod or perch		

DRY MEASURE

4 gills	= 1 pint	2 gallons	= 1 peck
2 pints	= 1 quart	4 pecks	= 1 bushel
4 quarts	= 1 gallon	8 bushels	= 1 quarter

LAND MEASURE

Land Measure is usually measured by Gunter's Chain, which consists of 100 links, and measures 66 feet (22 yards or 4 poles) in length.

62·724 square inches	= 1 square link		
2·295 ,, links	= 1 ,,	foot	
20·655 ,, ,,	= 1 ,,	yard	
625 ,, ,,	= 1 ,,	pole or perch	
40 ,, poles	= 1 ,,	rood	
4 ,, roods	= 1 acre (4840 yards)		
10 ,, chains	= 1 acre		

SQUARE MEASURE

144	square inches	= 1	square foot		
9	,, feet	= 1	,,	yard	
30¼	,, yards	= 1	,,	perch, rod or pole	
16	,, poles	= 1	,,	chain	
40	,, ,,	= 1	,,	rood	
4 roods		= 1 acre			
640 acres		= 1 mile			

FARMYARD MANURE—" DUNG SPREADING "

TABLE SHOWING NUMBER OF LOADS REQUIRED PER ACRE

Distance of heaps apart.	Heaps per load.			
	4.	5.	6.	8.
Yards.	Loads per acre.	Loads per acre.	Loads per acre.	Loads per acre.
5 × 5	48	38½	32	24
5 × 6	40	32	27	20
6 × 6	33	27	22½	17
6 × 7	29	23	19	14½
7 × 7	24½	20	16½	12
7 × 8	21½	17	14½	10½
8 × 8	19	15	12½	9½

To find the number of loads required for any other distances, divide 4840 (square yards = 1 acre) by the product of the two distances in yards between the heaps multiplied by the number of heaps per load.

Example.—Required the number of loads per acre, supposing each load to be divided into 7 heaps and the heaps 4 yards apart; then $4840 \div 4 \times 4 \times 7 = \frac{4840}{112} = 43\frac{1}{4}$, the number of loads required.

A TABLE OF MANURES WHICH MAY BE MIXED

Sulphate of ammonia with superphosphate.

,,	,,	,,	bone-meal.
,,	,,	,,	bone-flour.
,,	,,	,,	potash salts.
,,	,,	,,	guanos.
,,	,,	,,	compost.

Superphosphate with sulphate of ammonia.

,,	,,	bone-meal.
,,	,,	potash salts.
,,	,,	guanos.
	,,	compost.

Bone-meal and bone-flour with superphosphate.

| ,, | ,, | ,, | guanos. |

H

Bone-meal and bone-flour with sulphate of ammonia.
    ,,   ,,   ,,   nitrate of soda.
    ,,   ,,   ,,   compost.
    ,,   ,,   ,,   potash salts.
    ,,   ,,   ,,   basic slag.
    ,,   ,,   ,,   ground mineral phosphate.
    ,,   ,,   ,,   nitro chalk.

Basic slag with bone-meal.
    ,,   ,,   potash salts.
    ,,   ,,   nitrate of soda.

Guanos with bone-meal.
    ,,   ,,   potash salts.
    ,,   ,,   sulphate of ammonia.
    ,,   ,,   superphosphate.
    ,,   ,,   compost.

LIME, POTASH, PHOSPHORIC ACID AND NITROGEN CONTENT OF FERTILIZERS

Per cent.

Name.	Lime, CaO.	Potash, K_2O.	Phosphoric acid, P_2O_5.	Nitrogen, N.
Sulphate of ammonia :				
Ordinary	—	—	—	20
Neutral	—	—	—	20·6
Nitrate of soda	—	—	—	15·5
Nitrate of lime	16·8	—	—	13
Calcium cyanamide	60	—	—	20·6
Nitro-chalk	27	—	—	15·5
Nitrate of ammonia	—	—	—	35
Urea	—	—	—	46
Lunea saltpetre	—	—	—	25·5
Phosphate of ammonia	—	—	18·0–56·5	12·3–18·0
Superphosphate	—	—	13·7–18·3	—
Double superphosphate	—	—	40	—
Dissolved bones	—	—	15–16	2–3
Bone-meal	—	—	20–25	3·5–5·0
Bone-flour	—	—	27–28	0·75
Bone charcoal	—	—	32	0·8
Basic slag	2–8	—	9·0–17·5	—
Basic phosphate	—	—	13·5–23·0	—
Ground mineral phosphate	—	—	28–33	—
Potassic superphosphate	—	4	11·9	—
Sulphate of potash	—	48	—	—
Chloride of potash	—	50–55	—	—
Nitrate of potash	—	36·7	—	13·2
Kainit	—	14	—	—
Potash salts	—	20–30	—	—
Wood ashes	—	5–15	—	—
Flue dust	—	6	—	—
Peruvian guano	—	2·0–2·75	10–16	5–13
Seychelles guano	—	—	19	1
Fish guano	—	—	4–14	5–8
Meat meal	—	—	0·4	10·9

Name.	Lime, CaO.	Potash, K_2O.	Phosphoric acid, P_2O_5.	Nitrogen, N.
Dried blood . . .	—	—	1·2	11·5–14·0
Rape meal . . .	—	—	—	5–6
Hoof and hornmeal . .	—	—	—	12–14
Dissolved hidemeal . .	—	—	—	6·5
Castor meal . . .	—	—	—	4·5
Wool shoddy . . .	—	—	—	8
Decorticated cotton cake .	—	1·5	3	6·5
Soot	—	—	—	3·6
Farmyard manure, rotted .	0·7	0·5–1·5	0·25–0·75	0·5–1

SIZES OF FLOWER-POTS

Name of pot.	Diameter at top.	Depth.
	Inches.	Inches.
Thimbles	2	2
Thumbs	$2\frac{1}{2}$	$2\frac{1}{2}$
Sixties (60s) . . .	3	$3\frac{1}{2}$
Forty-eights (48s) . .	$4\frac{1}{2}$	5
Thirty-twos (32s) . .	6	6
Twenty-fours (24s) . .	$8\frac{1}{2}$	8
Sixteens (16s) . . .	$9\frac{1}{2}$	9
Twelves (12s) . . .	$11\frac{1}{2}$	10
Eights (8s) . . .	12	11
Sixes (6s)	13	12
Fours (4s) . . .	15	13
Twos (2s)	18	14

WEIGHT OF PRODUCE PER ACRE

Per sq. yard.	English acre, 4840 sq. yards.				Scotch acre, 6150 sq. yards.				Irish acre, 7840 sq. yards.	
lbs.	tons.	cwts.	st.	lbs.	tons.	cwts.	st.	lbs.	tons.	cwts.
1	2	3	1	10	2	14	7	4	3	10
2	4	6	3	6	5	9	6	8	7	0
3	6	9	5	2	8	4	5	12	10	10
4	8	12	6	12	10	19	5	2	14	0
5	10	16	0	8	13	14	4	6	17	10
6	12	19	2	4	16	9	3	10	21	0
7	15	2	4	0	19	4	3	0	24	10
8	17	5	5	10	21	19	2	4	28	0
9	19	8	7	6	24	14	1	8	31	10
10	21	12	1	2	27	9	0	12	35	0
11	23	15	2	12	30	4	0	2	38	10
12	25	18	4	8	32	18	7	6	42	0
13	28	1	6	4	35	13	6	10	45	10
14	30	5	0	0	38	8	6	0	49	0

A LIST OF INSTRUMENTS FOR LAYING OUT GARDEN PLOTS

Gunter's Chain. 66 feet = 22 yards = 4 perches. Divided into 100 links of 7·92 inches.

Garden Line or Reel.

Measuring Rod. 10 feet × 1¼ inches or 16½ feet long divided into 100 units for measuring by the pole or perch.

USES OF GARDEN TOOLS

Birch broom: for sweeping lawns and paths clear of leaves.

Crowbar: as a lever and for making holes for posts and stakes.

Dibber: for quicker transplanting, especially for cabbages, etc.

Dock digger: a useful tool for withdrawing deep roots of docks.

Drag: for market-garden work. Has three or more prongs.

Draw hoe: for drawing out drills, moving the soil.

Dutch hoe: for cutting off weeds on paths, beds, and smooth soils.

Fork, digging: has four or five flat prongs, heavier than the potato fork.

Fork, dung: for handling dung; has round prongs, usually four.

Fork, potato: has four or five flat prongs.

Grubbing axe: used for chopping out roots and suckers

Hammer: for general uses, nailing wall-trees.

Mallet: for driving stakes and wooden supports.

Mattock: for grubbing between roots, especially when trees are moved.

Pick: for breaking up hard surfaces and soils of strong nature.

Pickaxe: its sharp edge is advantageous when dealing with roots.

Rake: for preparing seed bed and generally " fining "
surface soil.

Rammer: for ramming soil hard against posts.

Rollers: for lawns and paths.

Shovel: used when sand, gravel or loose soil is moved.

Spade: for all garden uses.

Suckering iron: for removing suckers. Has a chisel
edge.

Trowel: for transplanting.

Turf beetle: for firming and making level new laid turves.

Turf cutter: for cutting turf.

Turfing iron: for removing turf in a uniform manner.

GERMINATION PERIOD OF VEGETABLE SEEDS

	Days.		Days.
Asparagus . .	14–21	Lettuce . .	6–10
Beans . . .	7–14	Melons (in heat) .	3–6
Beet . . .	10–18	Mustard . .	3–4
Broccoli . .	5–10	Onion . . .	10–16
Brussels sprouts .	5–10	Parsley . .	15–26
Cabbage . .	5–10	Parsnip . .	10–20
Carrot . .	12–18	Peas . . .	7–14
Cauliflower . .	5–10	Radish . .	3–6
Chicory . .	5–10	Savoy . .	5–10
Cress . . .	4–6	Spinach . .	7–10
Cucumbers (out-		Tomato (in heat) .	6–10
doors) . .	7–14	Turnip . .	4–10
Cucumbers (in		Vegetable marrow	
heat) . .	2–4	(outdoor) . .	7–14
Endive . .	5–14	Vegetable marrow	
Leeks . . .	10–14	(in heat) . .	3–5

A TABLE SHOWING THE APPROXIMATE
NUMBER OF PLANTS PRODUCED BY
ONE OUNCE OF SEED OF VEGETABLES
NAMED

Artichoke, globe	.	500	Endive	. . 1250
Asparagus	. .	800	Kale	. . . 3000
Beans, broad	.	14	Kohl rabi	. . 3000
„ French	.	150	Leek	. . . 1600
„ runner	.	125	Lettuce	. . 8000
Beet	. . .	1800	Marrow	. . 125
Broccoli	. .	2000	Melon	. . 500
Brussels sprouts	.	2000	Mustard	. . 2500
Cabbage	. .	2000	Onion	. . . 1250
Cardoon	. .	300	Parsley	. . 1400
Carrot	. .	3000	Parsnip	. . 750
Cauliflower	. .	2000	Peas	. . . 125
Celeriac	. .	3000	Pumpkin	. . 125
Celery	. . .	5000	Radish	. . 1000
Chard	. . .	1800	Rhubarb	. . 700
Chervil	. .	1500	Salsify	. . 500
Chicory	. .	1400	Savoy	. . . 2000
Chives	. .	1500	Swede	. . . 4000
Couve Tronchuda	.	2000	Tomato	. . 7500
Cucumber, ridge	.	1000	Turnip	. . 4000

A TABLE SHOWING THE AVERAGE
LONGEVITY OF VEGETABLE SEEDS

	Years.		Years.
Artichoke, globe .	3–4	Marjoram, sweet .	3
Asparagus . .	3	,, winter .	5
Basil . . .	8	Marrow . .	3
Beans . . .	3	Melon . .	5
Beet . . .	6	Mustard . .	4
Borage . .	8	Onion . . .	2
Broccoli . .	5	Parsley . .	3
Brussels sprouts .	5	Parsnip . .	2
Cabbage . .	5	Peas . . .	3
Cardoons . .	7	Pumpkin . .	3
Carrot . .	4	Radish . .	5
Cauliflower . .	5	Rhubarb . .	3
Celery . . .	4	Rosemary . .	4
Chard, Swiss .	4	Sage . . .	3
Cherril . .	1	Salsify . .	2
Chicory . .	8	Savory, summer or	
Chives . .	3	winter . .	3
Corn, sweet . .	3	Savoy . . .	5
Couve Tronchuda .	3	Scorzonera . .	2
Cress . . .	5	Seakale . .	1
Cucumber . .	6	Spinach (all varie-	
Endive . .	10	ties) . . .	5
Fennel . .	4	Swede . . .	5
Kale . . .	4	Thyme . .	3
Kohl rabi . .	5	Tomato . .	4
Leek . . .	3	Turnip . .	5
Lettuce . .	5		

POISON BAITS

1. For Leather Jackets and Slugs.

> 10 lb. bran
> $\frac{1}{2}$ lb. Paris green $\Big\}$ will cover $\frac{1}{2}$ acre.
> $\frac{1}{2}$ gallon of water

2. For Wood-Lice and Ants.

> 2 lb. sugar
> $\frac{1}{10}$ oz. tartaric acid $\Big\}$ mix and boil for $\frac{1}{2}$ hour
> 1 pint of water

> $\frac{1}{10}$ oz. sodium arsenate $\Big\}$ dissolve.
> 2 oz. hot water

Allow both to cool and mix thoroughly.
Add 3 oz. honey.

Dip small pieces of sponge in the liquid and place where required for ant control.

FORMULAE FOR FUNGICIDES

1. Bordeaux Mixture.

> (*a*) *For Potatoes* :

> > 1 lb. 6 oz. hydrated lime
> > 1 lb. 6 oz. powdered copper $\Big\}$ to 10 gallons
> >   sulphate   of water.

(*b*) *For Celery :*

    1½ lbs. hydrated lime

    1 lb. powdered copper sul-⎫ to 10 gallons

       phate   ⎭ of water.

(*c*) *For Fruit :*

    1¼ lbs. hydrated lime

    12 oz. powdered copper sul-⎫ to 10 gallons

       phate   ⎭ of water.

N.B.—Always dissolve the copper sulphate in a wooden or china vessel, and the whole mixture must be contained in a similar one.

2. LIME SULPHUR (used chiefly to control Scab in Apples).

    $\frac{1}{3}$ gallon or⎫

    $\frac{1}{6}$,,   or ⎪ in 10 gallons of water.

    $\frac{1}{8}$,,   or ⎪

    $\frac{1}{10}$,,   ⎭

These strengths vary according to circumstances.

3. COLLOIDAL COPPER. An alternative to Bordeaux. Proprietary name. Odourless.

4. COLLOIDAL SULPHUR. Sold under proprietary name. Odourless.

5. COPPER LIME DUST. Used on sulphur-shy plants.

6. SULPHUR DUST. Used where wet spraying is difficult.

FORMULAE FOR INSECTICIDES

1. ARSENATE OF LEAD.—Controls leaf-eating pests.

$\frac{1}{2}$ lb. paste
5 ozs. powder $\Big\}$ to 12 gallons of water.

POISONOUS

" Spreaders " are made under various proprietary names, and if used help to give a better cover.

N.B.—Never use soft soap with this mixture.

2. DERRIS. Controls many sucking insects.

Formula usually :—

$\frac{1}{4}$ lb. finely ground
$\frac{1}{2}$ lb. soft soap $\Big\}$ to 12 gallons of water.

NON-POISONOUS except to FISH

May be used as a dust.

3. NICOTINE. Controls most pests, but expensive.

$\frac{3}{4}$–1 oz. nicotine
8 oz. soft soap $\Big\}$ to 10 gallons of water.

POISONOUS

Nicotine dusts are available.
Most effective when applied in warm weather.

ANTIDOTES FOR POISONS

Poison.	*Antidote.*
Caustic potash Caustic soda	} Plenty of water containing lemon juice or vinegar.
Oil of vitriol Aqua fortis Oxalic acid	} Dissolve soap or magnesia in water, and take a little every two minutes.
Arsenic White precipitate Paris green London purple	} An emetic consisting of a table-spoonful each of mustard and salt; follow with butter, milk, or sweet oil.
Copper sulphate Corrosive sublimate Saltpetre Sugar of lead Red precipitate	} Large quantities of white of eggs or milk.

List of Illustrations

1. Land Girl ploughing the South Downs. © Jonathan Reeve JR1858b93p20 19391945.

2. Land Girl operating a 22-ton military bulldozer in the first stage of clearing land of trees for agriculture. © Jonathan Reeve JR1861b93p43T 19391945.

3. Preparing ground for tomatoes in a greenhouse in the market-gardening country near Evesham. © Jonathan Reeve JR1859b93p33 19391945.

4. Land Girl posing for the camera in full official kit. © Jonathan Reeve JR1748b92fp3 19391945.

5. Report form used to assess the progress of Land Girls. © Jonathan Reeve JR1750b92p96 19391945.

6. & 7. Treading the silo. One stage in the making of ensilage, a method of preserving green fodder. © Jonathan Reeve JR1864b93p59 19391945 and © Jonathan Reeve JR1772b92pic20 19391945.

8. Music and lyrics to Back to the Land, the Land Army song. © Jonathan Reeve JR1752b92p112 19391945.

9. Land Girl laying hedges. © Jonathan Reeve JR1773b92pic21 19391945.

10, 11, 12, & 13. Harvest time. © Jonathan Reeve JR1778b92pic26 19391945, © Jonathan Reeve JR1776b92pic24 19391945, © Jonathan Reeve JR1206b70fp39T 19391945 and © Jonathan Reeve JR1869b93p91T 19391945.

14. & 15. Land Girls caring for livestock. © Jonathan Reeve JR1796b92pic44 19391945 and © Jonathan Reeve JR1797b92pic45 19391945.

16. & 17. Land Girls caring for livestock. © Jonathan Reeve JR1759b92pic7 19391945 and © Jonathan Reeve JR1763b92pic11 19391945.

18. Digging ditches. © Jonathan Reeve JR1788b92pic36 19391945.

19, 20, 21, 22 & 23. The Land Army Timber Corps at work. © Jonathan Reeve JR1432b70fp39B 19391945, © Jonathan Reeve JR1800b92pic48 19391945, © Jonathan Reeve JR1803b92pic51 19391945, © Jonathan Reeve JR1801b92pic49 19391945 and © Jonathan Reeve JR1805b92pic53 19391945.

24. Picking apples. © Jonathan Reeve JR1790b92pic38 19391945.

25. Proud Land Girl with pitch-fork in hand. © Jonathan Reeve JR1205b70fp38 19391945.

Also available from Amberley Publishing

How to fly the legendary fighter plane in combat using the manuals and instructions supplied by the RAF during the Second World War

An amazing array of leaflets, books and manuals were issued by the War Office during the Second World War to aid pilots in flying the Supermarine Spitfire, here for the first time they are collated into a single book with the original 1940s setting. An introduction is supplied by expert aviation historian Dilip Sarkar. Other sections include aircraft recognition, how to act as an RAF officer, bailing out etc.

£9.99 Paperback
40 illustrations
264 pages
978-1-84868-436-2

Available from all good bookshops or to order direct
Please call **01285-760-030**
www.amberleybooks.com

25. Proud Land Girl with pitch-fork in hand.